CW00371420

Conviction
Violence, culture
and a shared public service agenda

John Carnochan

C|C|W|B press

First published by Argyll Publishing in 2015.

New edition published in 2016 by CCWB Press
Reprinted 2018

This edition 2021

Centre for Confidence and Well-being.
Registered Office Abercorn House,
79 Renfrew Rd, Paisley, PA3 4DA

A catalogue record of this book is available from the British Library

ISBN 978 1 9160094 3 1

Printing: Bell & Bain Ltd., Glasgow

Postcards from Scotland

Series editor: Carol Craig

Advisory group:
Professor Phil Hanlon, Chair,
Centre for Confidence and Well-being;
Fred Shedden

Contents

Acknowledgements

I'd like to thank a few people who have inspired, encouraged and supported me in writing this book and more generally on my journey over the past ten years. First, Willie Rae for his vision, his confidence and his guidance, without him I would have retired in 2004 and be playing better golf. Harry Burns, Phil Hanlon, Alan Sinclair, Martin Johnston and Carol Craig who listened and made me think differently but mostly for confirming we were on the right lines; Carol too for guiding me through the process of writing and helping me tell the story. All the team past and present at the Violence Reduction Unit (VRU), they are delivering the extraordinary every day and changing lives. The countless ordinary people, professional, academic and committed people here in Scotland and elsewhere working heroically everyday to make things better.

Mostly I want to thank Karyn McCluskey who is one of the smartest, most passionate and most tenacious people I know. I've worked with some great cops during my forty years in the police and she is as good as the very best of them.

It's been a great journey full of surprise, disappointment and joy. We also had a lot of laughs, and it's not over yet.

Foreword [to 2021 edition] by James Mitchell

A less travelled road

This book is about a journey. A journey that started when a senior police officer was asked to produce a Homicide Reduction Strategy in a place that had an appalling record for violent crime. It would have been easy to choose the easy road, offer more of the same dressed up as something different. But a less travelled road was chosen.

John Carnochan had built a successful career as a police officer and could have coasted into retirement knowing that he had made his contribution to public service. But the gruesome Ground Hog Day of seeing brown bags with 'blooded stained clothing' each morning as he came into work told him that enforcement could only be part of the response to violence. Prevention was others' responsibility. Embedding prevention thinking into policing and the wider justice sector was not without its challenges.

There are many parts to the story of how this was done. Those with responsibility took a risk. Sir Willie Rae, Strathclyde's Chief Constable, was open-minded and trusting. It helped that John had considerable experience. No number of academic treatises on prevention could make up for the street credibility he had.

Partnership was a key. Identifying like-minded and focused support was important and Karyn McCluskey certainly provided that. This formidable team sought out others, analysed the evidence and showed the same openness to ideas that the Chief Constable had shown. The approach adopted required, in John's words, 'real partnerships with those working in education, social work, prisons, courts, health and other organisations or individuals with a genuine interest in reducing violence'. Achieving that was no picnic.

The Violence Reduction Unit (VRU) that was set up might easily have become one of those gestures that allowed senior policy makers to claim to be doing something. But establishing the VRU was only one step on the road. The VRU has been a remarkable achievement and one impossible to quantify. Much policy output is expected to meet targets, to demonstrate (by which is usually meant *quantify*) success. But often what counts can't be counted. This book offers an alternative, more powerful, more human way of looking at outcomes.

David's story is hugely important. What can never be known are the many lives affected by the VRU and other preventative approaches. The financial cost of the numerous interventions over David's short life time recounted in these pages would have to be multiplied by an unknown number but we can be sure the costs of 'failure demand' are huge. And that is only the financial saving. The more important human cost raises the question of what-might-have-been. What road might have been taken for so many whose lives were affected directly and indirectly by violence? And that is the real loss.

John Carnochan writes honestly. As he says, it is 'not easy to empathise with David the murderer, but David's behaviour is a consequence of his life, particularly his early life' but empathy and understanding are key. 'He needed help when he was the victim of violence and neglect, when his mother was the victim of violence from his dad. But we didn't help David the baby or David the child so it's hardly surprising that we don't help David the murderer. But what about David the dad?' This is a story of empathetic, collaborative, preventative, efficient work.

It would be wrong to suggest that the battle to place prevention at the heart of policing, far less across all public services, has been won. But this story contributed to achieving the most difficult part of any journey. The first steps are always the most difficult. John quotes Machiavelli:

> 'There is nothing more difficult to carry out, nor more doubtful of success, nor more dangerous to conduct than to initiate a new order of things. For the reformer has enemies in all who profit by the old order and only lukewarm defenders in all those who profit by the new order.'

Not so long ago, even suggesting that prevention should be a policing function was dismissed. Today, it is understood as a key responsibility. There may be a rhetoric-reality gap in prevention across our public services but getting it on the agenda makes it possible to question, challenge and demand that the gap is closed.

There is a tendency in politics to view policy making as a mechanical exercise. Passing a piece of legislation or making a Ministerial statement is often seen as like pulling a lever that will deliver some desired outcome. Reality is far messier and more complex. Policies are meaningless unless and until they have effect in our communities. The failure to take this into account leads to policy failure and frustration. Perversely, such failure can in turn lead to even more lever pulling at the centre. This is particularly true when it comes to what are often referred to as 'wicked problems'. Wicked problems are not easily solved – indeed cannot be eradicated. The very term 'problem' is itself problematic. We are talking about people and, as is made abundantly clear in this book, relationships. These relationships are complex, multi-disciplinary and require partnership and empathy to avoid duplication or, worst of all, competing and contradictory understandings of what needs to be done.

Violence cannot be eradicated like smallpox. Wicked problems need to be *re*-solved, solved on a daily basis and that requires a very different approach as is powerfully articulated here. There is much that is remarkable about this book and while it would be a mistake to attempt to replicate the approach in its entirety elsewhere, there is plenty to stimulate, provoke and learn from for anyone interested in policy making and delivering public services. There is no magic bullet or lever to be pulled and there can be no final resolution. There is always more to learn, more opportunities to improve. This is a work in progress. The VRU is, as all the best organisations, a learning institution.

John Carnochan's book brings to mind Robert Frost's poem *The Road Not Taken*. John himself took the road less travelled and 'that has made all the difference'. We have a long way to go on this road but this book should inspire us on that journey.

James Mitchell,
Professor of Public Policy, University of Edinburgh
July 2021

Foreword [to 2015 edition] by Carol Craig

This book is not an analysis of violence or a list of policy recommendations for how to reduce it. It is much more insightful, and useful, than that. *Conviction* is about experience in the real world. It's about what works. It's also about the fundamental importance of commitment, perseverance, partnership and caring.

In some respects *Conviction* is John Carnochan's story. It starts when he is a Detective Superintendent working in the CID in Lanarkshire. Prior to this he had twenty-seven years' experience working in areas of Glasgow with high murder rates. Most of these murders were the result of feuding gangs. The violence was largely 'recreational' – it was what they did. Rather than questioning why this was the case, John, his colleagues and local residents accepted that this was a fact of life.

But this complacency was about to change. Under the enlightened 'command and convince' leadership of Sir Willie Rae, John was appointed head of the new Violence Reduction Unit (VRU). With the slogan 'violence is preventable – not inevitable' John and his colleagues set about finding allies and looking for ideas on how they could stop the violence.

The VRU has been, and continues to be, spectacularly successful. The Scottish murder rate has halved in the last decade. Violence has fallen in most Western countries but the Scottish figures are much more dramatic and, as you will see in this book, attributable to the VRU's activities.

Indeed the reduction in the Scottish violence figures has attracted considerable media attention throughout the UK. They regularly profile the VRU and the inspirational figures who are integral to the story. John and his colleague Karyn McLuskey, who now leads the Unit, are also much in demand as presenters at conferences – not just in Scotland but internationally as there is so much interest in their success story.

However, *Conviction* takes us into new territory. The book sets out in detail how the VRU managed to reduce Scotland's murder rate – particularly those related to youth gangs. In many places *Conviction* reads like a voyage of discovery. It describes how the VRU worked and the ideas and theories which influenced them.

One thing repeatedly struck me as I read this book – the VRU would have achieved little if they had tried to cover up the extent of the problem they were grappling with. Instead they kept telling people how bad Scotland's violence figures were in comparison with other countries. They also repeatedly said that these figures were underestimates as many serious injuries went unreported. In short, they were incredibly open – a virtue rarely seen in public bodies.

But alongside this willingness to accept the sheer extent of the problem was the VRU's confidence and optimism that things could change – that various public agencies could work together in different ways and save lives.

John and his colleagues inspired people to think that change was really possible. And, as you are about to see, they were right.

Carol Craig
Series Editor, Postcards from Scotland

CHAPTER 1

Fire Fighting

In 2000 James Garbarino, an American psychologist and crime expert, came to Scotland to speak at a conference in Hamilton, South Lanarkshire. His audience was mostly social workers and criminal justice people, including a few cops. During his talk Garbarino suggested that if Scottish males had access to guns then the murder rate in Scotland would match that of South Bronx in New York or the inner city area of Detroit. This was not a welcome comparison as both areas at that time had a notorious reputation for violence. Garbarino also noted that, even without access to guns, young Scottish men were killing one another at a rate that was four times greater than the equivalent rates for England or Wales.

Garbarino also told his audience that he put this high level of violence down to the fact that we Scots are always very quick to take offence and can even respond to small, personal insults with violence.

If all that wasn't bad enough, Garbarino then went on to suggest that the Scots were net exporters of violence. He argued that there was strong evidence to suggest that it was Scottish immigrants who started and encouraged the high levels of interpersonal violence in the United States. It was the Scots, Garbarino claimed, who were obsessed by respect and who spread this obsession to many American communities. According to our speaker, New Zealand's high violence figures can also be traced to the country's Scottish roots.

Garbarino is not the only academic who believes that Scots have had a significant influence on the levels of violence in the USA. For example, the cultural conservative thinker William Lind also argues that the early Scots immigrants, who mostly settled in the Southern States, were violent and prone to feuding.

I wasn't at the conference but I heard from those who attended that Garbarino's opinion provoked a strong response. It is easy to see why they may have been shocked by his thesis. Some suggested that his view of Scottish men had simply been drawn from the stereotypical Scottish male in Hollywood films and bore little resemblance to reality.

I suspect that their disquiet was compounded by the fact that here was an American telling a Scottish audience in Scotland that their country was not only violent but that their ancestors had exported that violent feuding culture to other parts of the world. No one responded violently even though some thought his comments disrespectful. But I am aware that even now when Garbarino's name is mentioned, it touches a nerve for those who were there that day.

Personally I think there is something in Garbarino's thesis. I think that Scots are thrawn, that we take offence easily and that we never forget. Many young boys in Scotland are usually schooled by their parents not to allow anyone to disrespect them. So if a young boy runs home to his mum crying because someone has hit him, she is very likely to give him a cuddle then send him out to find his assailant and get revenge. She will encourage him to fight 'his own battles' and to ensure that he gets respect. At least that is what it is like in areas in Scotland which have the worst violence.

Violence west of Scotland style

While Garbarino was talking to his audience in Hamilton, I was about five miles away in Motherwell Police Office. If I had been present I suspect I would have responded in much the same way as the rest of the audience with a mixture of shock, disbelief and indignation.

I was a Detective Superintendent, head of the Criminal Investigation Department (CID) in Lanarkshire. I had been a police officer for twenty-seven years and spent the majority of my career working in the CID, mostly in Glasgow. I had always worked in busy areas, including Easterhouse, Springburn and Maryhill where there were high levels of recorded crime, including interpersonal violence, domestic violence, gang related violence and drug abuse.

I never consciously thought about why there was so much violence. I just presumed that's what it was like and that it was my job to deal with it. This meant investigating incidents after they had occurred. I seldom, if ever, made any real comparisons with other areas and if I did I simply thought that the police officers who worked there were not as busy as me.

Looking back I can see that I had been so busy *fire fighting* I had not taken any time to consider how the *fires* started or even why there were so many of them. What's more I wasn't alone; that was how all my colleagues thought as well.

Indeed those of us in the CID saw our contribution to prevention as limited to arresting violent perpetrators for crimes they had already committed thus preventing them from committing more crimes, at least while they were in prison.

I also dealt in certainties. I knew that knives and alcohol played a significant part in most violent incidents. I knew it was mostly young men that we arrested or dealt with as offenders and victims. I knew that a lot of these young men carried facial scars inflicted during some encounter with some other young man from a different area. These facial scars were known as 'chib' marks and we dealt with lots of young men who had been 'chibbed'.

When I worked in Easterhouse in the late 80s, we were always dealing with high levels of violent crimes, gang fights and drugs. There were over fifty territorial youth gangs in the greater Easterhouse area and they fought each other most weekends at various boundaries between their territories. They would use anything as a weapon: bricks or sticks, for example, and the more organised would have baseball bats, knives or machetes or even samurai swords. The injuries they inflicted on each other were usually significant and occasionally fatal.

This territorialism also meant that young gang members would often carry a weapon, usually a kitchen knife, whenever they left the house. The knife was 'just for protection' in case they came across members of a rival gang. The feuds between the gangs were constant and no one could tell us exactly why they disliked each other so much that they would fight and inflict horrific injuries. Indeed it is best to describe the fighting as recreational: it was what they did, what they had always done. What's more, so had their dads and their big brothers. In a word, it was *normal*.

What was continually striking was gang members' loyalty to their friends. They would fight with them and fight for them; they would put themselves at risk of serious injury or arrest. In other circumstances their loyalty would have been deemed worthy and deserving of reward. Indeed soldiers fighting in wars receive medals for such behaviour.

Incidents

Most of the violence occurred in the evenings and at weekends. The nightshifts could be very busy and the detectives working this shift carried out the initial investigation of reported incidents. They then prepared a summary of the incidents, and a list of the enquiries they had completed together with a list of things still outstanding. They then left this information for the day shift team so they could complete the enquiries.

The initial investigations involved interviewing any witnesses including medical staff who treated the victim. These statements were left for the dayshift. In some instances the accused had been arrested at the time of the incident and was in custody. Further enquiries were generally needed before the case could be prepared for submission to the Procurator Fiscal. The nightshift also seized any relevant productions, weapons used, CCTV tapes and the blood stained clothing from the victim. They then submitted all this for forensic examination.

In order to ensure the blood stained clothing was preserved for examination, nightshift staff labeled and placed it in brown paper bags. If the stained clothing was kept in a plastic bag the blood deteriorated thus making forensic examination impossible. Some nights the nightshift team had to deal with several violent incidents and seized countless productions including blood stained items, like clothing. The brown paper bags were then grouped together around the office and on some memorably busy weekends the nightshift even used the stairs to keep productions together.

It was always very depressing to start your shift at 8am and have to pick your way past brown paper bags on the stairs. The dayshift on Saturdays and Sundays were so busy as a result of night time violence that they became known in the CID as a 'brown bag day'. Those of us who worked there at that time still sometimes refer to any busy day, anywhere, as a 'brown bag day'. Unfortunately while I was working in the west of Scotland I saw too many brown bag days.

Not all the violence we dealt with happened on the streets and not all involved gangs. There were also very violent incidents at house parties where all the victims, the witnesses and the offenders were usually drunk. Taking statements about what happened at these parties was always a challenge. It was not uncommon on brown bag days to find drunken witnesses asleep in the waiting room or an interview room. They would usually sleep off the alcohol and then we interviewed them in the morning or when they had sobered up enough to remember what had happened. Some never remembered.

Everyone seemed to accept the high level of violence that existed as normal, even inevitable. We just thought it had always been like this and, while we never said so aloud, I'm certain most of us also believed that it would always remain like this. This was not only the view of the police who worked in Easterhouse but also most of the people who lived there. It is as if we had all reached an unspoken agreement that it was how life was if you lived there.

Many detectives viewed working in these areas as a real badge of honour; if you could work there you could work anywhere. The experience gained was unrivalled anywhere and there was something of a 'snobbery' when we met colleagues from less violent areas. When we met officers from other force areas there was always a certain perverse pride in saying you worked in Easterhouse. Everyone knew about Easterhouse and how violent it was and so there was an unspoken assumption that if you worked there you were good at what you did.

Many of the residents in places like Easterhouse also accepted the gang fighting and violence as normal, inevitable and essentially unstoppable. We regularly came across evidence of an intergenerational connection in some families where the sons of gang members were now in the same gang as their fathers. This continuity also reinforced the view that it was normal and part of every day life.

I recall one Saturday morning going to the house of a young boy who had committed a serious assault the night before. The nightshift had been so busy working on this incident and other incidents that they had no time to go and arrest him. So this became my job.

The boy was fifteen years old and I knew both him and his family. When I arrived at his house his mother told me he wasn't in and even invited me into the house to confirm that she was telling the truth. I asked her where he might be and when she had last seen him. She replied that she had no idea where he would be and that she had last seen him about 6pm the previous night when 'he had gone to meet his pals and go gang fighting.' She stated this in such a matter of fact tone and seemed to have no awareness of how strange or absurd the statement sounded. His dad had also been a member of the same gang in his day; unsurprisingly he sat there in silence.

Good at what we did

In these days Strathclyde Police had an excellent reputation particularly in relation to murder enquiries. Our detection rate was always around 98–99 per cent. No doubt this was why officers from other forces around the UK and beyond would visit us to learn from our investigation methods and our outstanding detection rate. At that time it never occurred to me that one of the reasons we were so good at investigating murders was because we had so many of them. But it did occur to me even then that we were catching the feckless and the stupid. Thankfully complex murder enquiries only came along now and again and most investigations were relatively straightforward and solved within a few days. Since investigating a murder largely draws on technical skills, experience and practice help considerably.

Easterhouse was not the only area of Glasgow with high levels of violence and large numbers of young men involved in street gangs; other areas of Strathclyde had the same problems. What's more, every other area of Scotland had violent crime, though perhaps not on the scale or volume of Strathclyde and Glasgow. In short, violence was not an issue confined to the west of Scotland or indeed to Glasgow. In 2003 there were 108 murders recorded in Scotland and of these 73 occurred in Strathclyde and 35 elsewhere in Scotland. Glasgow had 30 murders that year, Aberdeen 6 and Edinburgh 5. Almost half of all murders were committed using a knife or sharp instrument and that held true, not just in Glasgow, but all areas of Scotland.

Strathclyde Police, like every other force in the UK, police with consent of the communities they serve. Prevention is a legitimate function of the police but we were so busy responding to the everyday violence that we devoted very little time, energy or thought to how we might prevent violence from happening. Of course, there were crime prevention departments but they were very small units and they concentrated on the physical security of property such as locks and alarms and bars on windows. If they did speak about personal safety it would be about locks and alarms and bars on windows.

A step change

By 2004 I was Deputy Head of CID Operations and working at Force Headquarters in Glasgow. Part of my role there was to ensure that the Chief Constable and his Command team received daily briefings concerning incidents of serious crime. Serious crime included murder, suicide, rape, drug deaths, and all significant drug recoveries. I also had to provide updates on ongoing police operations. My role also meant that I had to ensure that all major investigations were adequately resourced and managed.

Fortunately for me, and the unfolding story, the Chief Constable in Strathclyde at this time was Willie Rae – soon to become Sir Willie Rae. He was a very thoughtful, inclusive and modest man who actively encouraged innovation and collaboration. He was not a 'command and control' style of leader. He believed in 'command and convince.'

During 2004 some people working in the media were very vocal about Strathclyde's high murder levels. Several newspapers were demanding to know what the police were doing, and some newspapers were even more specific in asking what the Chief Constable was doing about the high levels of murder. In truth what we were doing was what police everywhere had always being doing: we were reacting and responding to murders *after* they had been committed. Almost all of our efforts were focused on the investigation and conviction process and we devoted almost no thought or effort into preventing them from happening.

Previous Chief Constables had introduced initiatives focused on violence. These initiatives often had names like 'Operation Blade'. They could involve a weapons amnesty and increased policing in identified areas. Sometimes such initiatives did make a difference when they were in force but they were never sustained and the impact and gains were quickly lost.

Thanks to Willie Rae I had been tasked with producing a Homicide Reduction Strategy. Such strategies were all the rage around the UK with police forces of a similar size to Strathclyde's.

Like every other UK police force at the time Strathclyde was establishing a new intelligence structure called the National Intelligence Model or NIM. This model was about smarter policing. Basically those of us in the police had realised that we required a better understanding of exactly what we did, exactly why we did it and exactly how we did it. Intelligence analysts were at the heart of the model. They were smart people who used data, including crime statistics, to examine crime trends locally and nationally. They produced evaluations of operational outcomes and helped police to understand better what was going on in their area and so help shape how they might operate more effectively. In Strathclyde the principal analyst employed to create this new structure was Karyn McCluskey.

Karyn had worked in several English police forces before joining Strathclyde and she was not only a fresh pair of eyes but also a very smart individual and a very savvy analyst. She still is.

Karyn and I began discussing the issue of violence and what we could do about it.

Analysis requires data to help understand the problem. For policing it's reported crime figures which are used universally as the measure of all things related to crime. But the problem is that such figures are notoriously inaccurate. For a start, not all crimes are reported and even when a crime is reported the police do not always record the incident as a 'crime'. This means it is almost impossible to produce any meaningful and accurate baseline figures. What's more, criminal justice experts are always amending, adjusting or altering crime classifications and so making comparisons, between different areas over time, almost meaningless. So it is easy to see how crime figures reflect police activity rather the actual levels of crime experienced by individuals and communities. This is particularly true in relation to violent crime.

However, there is one category of violent crime that is usually accurate – homicide or, as we prefer to say in Scotland, murder. It is also the most serious of crimes and attracts the most media attention.

In 2004 an Accident and Emergency doctor in Glasgow conducted a small-scale study of presentations to A&E departments across the city. During April he collated the number of people who presented at A&E departments in Glasgow as a result of being a victim of violence. This data provided a snapshot of the levels of serious violence in the city. This study allowed us to compare the data he had collected with the number of crimes of violence reported to the police over the same period of time. We discovered that only between 33–50 per cent of those attending A&E as a victim of violence were reporting the crime to the police. This was a critically important finding as it meant that the crime figures were completely inaccurate and that the level of violence was much higher than we had first thought.

What was even more alarming about this study was the reasons victims gave for not reporting the incidents to the police. They said they were too afraid; would 'sort it' themselves; or didn't think the police could do anything.

I found the extent of under-reporting and the reasons for it both surprising and shocking. If people were going to 'sort it' themselves that meant more violence; if they didn't think the police could do anything then that was damaging to our policing by consent ethos. The thought that people were too afraid to report the violent crime to the police was disturbing.

In August 2004 Karyn tasked the newly formed Strategic Analysis Unit at Force Headquarters to produce a violent crime reduction strategy. This strategy was to have a twin focus. First it was to focus on education and the delivery of a long-term awareness programme about violence and weapons aimed at school children between the age of six and sixteen. The second focus was on enforcement and aimed to manage and contain those individuals who had already embarked on a lifestyle where violent crime and weapon carrying had become established behaviour.

We realised quickly that any strategy that focused exclusively on homicide would likely fail. We came to this conclusion as we already knew that the overwhelming number of homicides we were dealing with were not intentional homicides. There was no doubt that the violence was intentional but the outcome was happenstance – a stab wound to the upper torso where one centimeter left or right could be the difference between life and death. The victims and the perpetrators were usually male, knew each other and were living in our most deprived areas. They would be involved in lots of fighting and across their violent careers they would each play the role of victim and perpetrator, winner and loser. In most incidents 'losing' meant stitches and a scar; but for some losing meant death and winning meant a life sentence.

I had investigated enough murders to know that we were seldom dealing with cunning criminals. Yes we had our share of them but we were usually dealing with the feckless and the stupid. What's more, the similarities between the personal circumstances of the victim and the murderer were always striking and which of the two participants in a fatal fight became the victim and which became the accused was often random. The affect on both families too was also very similar. It was often fate that decided which family would be visiting their son's grave and which would be visiting their son in prison.

This realisation helped us make our first decision: we had to focus all our efforts on reducing violence not just murder. If we were successful then murder rates would automatically come down.

Setting up the unit

One of the problems we identified fairly early on in our discussions was that criminal justice services were seen by some politicians and much of the media as a service of first resort. In other words, they thought that punishment was the deterrent. A popular but, from my point of view, hollow mantra in society at large is that we need to be 'tough on crime' and give stiffer sentences to those caught.

So for a variety of reasons prevention was not particularly high on the policing agenda or indeed anyone's agenda. Violence was a crime and crime was a matter for the police. Some senior police officers subscribed to this view and continually argued that crime would be reduced if they had more cops, more powers, and more resources. Luckily Willie Rae was not one of those who held this narrow and limiting view of crime. He understood that crime in general, and violence in particular, is a complex problem that requires a far more comprehensive response than just more cops and longer sentences.

Karyn and I met with Willie Rae to speak to him about our findings and our thoughts on how we might bring about sustainable reductions in violent crime. I don't think we were telling him anything he did not already know.

We suggested that any plan or strategy would have to be innovative and radical. There was no point in doing more of the same because it was evident that it wouldn't work in the long term. Our new strategy required real partnerships with those working in education, social work, prisons, courts, health and other organisations or individuals with a genuine interest in reducing violence.

We concluded that meeting with Sir Willie by saying that he should get three or four smart people and lock them in a room for a few months until they came up with a plan. He replied: 'Good, go and find another two people and a room, then come back to me with the plan.' Karyn immediately began calling him 'Nike' – 'just do it'.

We found a couple of smart heads, one a Detective Sergeant and the other a senior analyst. Then we found an empty room with several blank white boards and started to fill them with lists of things to do. They were long lists.

We also decided on a name for the team: the Violence Reduction Unit. We made the conscious decision not to include the word 'crime' in our title since this would signal to everyone that what we were dealing with was an issue solely for the police and criminal justice. Even at this very early stage in the journey we knew this not to be true. We also decided on 'reduction' as opposed to eradication; there is a fine line between vision and hallucination.

We didn't have an allocated budget as such but Willie Rae had made money available to the departments we had come from to backfill our vacated posts. We of course had negotiated with the department heads to absorb the cost of backfilling within their departmental budgets; this gave us a very reasonable working budget. We realised that we could only spend the money once, so we were determined to spend it wisely and not on overtime to do more of the same.

We adopted the strap line 'Violence is preventable – not inevitable' and we started to develop our thinking, our knowledge and our understanding of violence and most importantly what to do about it.

CHAPTER 2
The quest for evidence

By August 2004 we were ensconced in our temporary office in Force Headquarters in Glasgow. It was a room maintained in a state of readiness for emergencies and well equipped with the usual office stuff. But it had no windows, and wasn't a very invigorating working environment so we called it the 'dunny'. The room was also a powerful incentive to get out and about and meet people, and we did.

We had no real plan, we weren't sure what we wanted to do and we had even less of an idea of how we might do it. We were not 'business' people. We did not have an MBA between us so we had no project plan, no project initiation document, and no established milestones. (Athough I think I once attended a one day course on project management.) But one thing was clear: while we didn't know what had to be done we knew that it had to be different from what we had been doing.

On reflection I can see that this lack of direction was to our advantage. After all we came from the police, which is in effect a crisis organisation. This means that we work best in a crisis, and that the longer we have to plan for something the more likely it will be over-engineered and the less likely it will deliver results. So we came at the challenge like police, and ironically in the same way that we would have approached any murder enquiry: find out what had happened, establish what we know and follow the evidence, wherever it may lead. Our only hypothesis was that violence was preventable not inevitable.

Like any murder enquiry we wanted more information, more evidence. We needed to identify witnesses – people with information relevant to our task – and speak to them to help build a better picture. We had access to research reports and evaluation reports of things that had worked elsewhere.

Some important influences

In 2005 we met George Hosking, the CEO of the WAVE Trust (World Alternatives to Violence) when he was speaking at a conference. George had conducted a comprehensive literature review on violence and produced a very good report called 'violence and what to do about it.' His conclusion, in summary, is that a lack of empathy has a significant impact on the levels of violence and that by tackling child abuse and neglect, violence would be reduced.

We met with George on several occasions and his work helped broaden our knowledge and understanding of violence prevention. He was the first person we had encountered who spoke about the importance of the early years.

After meeting with George we met with Mary Gordon a Canadian who had created a programme in her own country called 'Roots of Empathy'. Mary is an educator who believes that the solution to bullying and anti-social behaviour lies within a child's natural sense of caring and compassion. Her programme involves pupils in primary school interacting with babies and their mums. By doing this the children observe the relationship between mothers and their babies and see how the babies learn and communicate.

It is a very successful programme and has now been introduced into Scotland. In fact it is supported by the Scottish Government and there is at least one Roots of Empathy school in every local authority.

As a result of encountering the work of the WAVE Trust and Roots of Empathy I began to develop my own views. I don't think we learn how to be violent I think we learn how not be violent. We learn how to communicate, negotiate, compromise, and solve problems and so violence becomes the last option on our tactical options menu. These human attributes allow us to judge risk and to make good decisions about ourselves: they help us navigate life and establish and maintain relationships and principal among them is empathy, the glue that holds society together.

We also learned about an American health project often referred to as the ACE Study and it too had a big impact on our thinking. This large-scale research study examined 17,000 adults' responses to questions about childhood abuse and household dysfunction. The questionnaire also asked respondents to outline their current mental and physical health. Individuals scored one point for each adverse experience they recalled. There were eight adverse experiences covering matters such as neglect, physical and emotional abuse, parental separation and divorce and household dysfunction such as domestic violence and substance misuse. Its conclusions were startling. It showed a 'powerful relationship' between what happened to us as children and our future mental and physical health. The more adverse childhood experiences people reported, the more likely they were to have heart disease, bronchitis, cancer, stroke, diabetes, skeletal fractures, liver disease and poor health as an adult.

Some of the findings were particularly relevant to the work we were doing in Scotland with its high incidence of drugs and suicide. For example, the study showed that a male who gains six points on the ACE questionnaire has a 4,600 per cent increase in the likelihood of using heroin intravenously than another who scored zero. Those with high ACE scores are at much higher risk (3,000–5,100 per cent) of committing suicide.

Humans can adapt to most environments, both good and bad. If you are a child born into an environment that is aggressive and violent and where there is neglect and lack of consistency you are likely to survive but there will be a cost and not just to your long term physical and mental health. It will be noticed when you start nursery and you can't play with other children. You don't speak much because no one has spoken to you, you won't share, and you respond with aggression to most situations.

When you begin primary school your behaviour will no doubt continue to alienate you from the other children. You will gain a reputation for being 'a bad boy', a problem. While you are being 'bad' you will, of course, not be able to learn all the good stuff the teacher is passing on to the other children. You won't learn to read and write or count as well as them. You will become further set apart.

By the time you arrive at secondary school, your behaviour will be getting progressively worse and while the other children are continuing to learn you will be getting further detached and separated from them. You will start to get involved in more risky behaviour. You may try drugs, alcohol or violence. You'll be attending school less and less, and you may even be excluded. You'll begin to get into trouble with the police, you may end up with previous convictions, or become an alcoholic or a drug addict just as the ACE study suggests. The downward spiral that started before you were born will continue throughout your life.

Such young men seldom get a job, seldom stay in a relationship, and will likely die young. They will have drawn heavily on public services for most of their lives.

I have spent most of my professional life locking up young men like this. Young men who were mostly feckless and stupid, young men who could barely string half a dozen words together and who seldom ventured far from their home territory. When they spoke to anyone there was only minimal eye contact, not unusual when you consider the level of violence that for many existed everywhere in their lives. The phrase 'what are you looking at', is usually a challenge and precursor to violence. And it is easy to see why so many young men and women learned not to look at other people and they definitely learned not to stare.

One of the reports which had the biggest impact on us in these days was from the World Health Organisation (WHO). We discovered that in 1996, at the 49th World Health Assembly, the World Health Organisation declared violence 'a major and growing public health concern around the world' and in 2002 WHO published a major report on violence. This authoritative report clearly defined violence as a public health issue. We found this very interesting and I confess my initial thought was to give the problem to health professionals as soon as possible. Of course, this was not an option as this is not how things work in the real world.

One of the immediate and obvious benefits of adopting a public health approach to reducing and preventing violence was that we acquired a whole new lexicon of words to describe the problem and define the cure and I'll explore some of these in the following section. All that matters here is that the 2002 WHO report categorised different types of violence from interpersonal violence to collective violence (war). It also argued that violence can be defined to include everything from bullying to suicide. In their view, suicide is 'self directed' violence. I found this scary as alongside the stabbings and violent crime in Scotland we have also have a worrying level of suicide. Indeed at that time we had eight suicides for every murder.

The public health methodology also provided a clear scientific model with which to tackle violence. This fitted perfectly into our investigative approach to the challenge. This model has four elements:

    1 Understand the scale of the problem.

    2 Understand why it occurs.

    3 Find out what works to prevent it.

    4 Scale up what works.

Scale of the problem

In Scotland it was easy to access reported crime figures for Strathclyde as well as Scottish crime statistics. Here are the violence statistics for Scotland in 2004/05:

Murders	142
Attempted Murders	828
Serious Assaults	6,775
Simple Assaults	73,711

These figures were very similar to those of previous years and let's not forget the levels of under-reporting. We know from research that only 30 to 50 per cent of those treated at hospital for a violence related injury will report it to the police. If we apply what we know about under-reporting to the attempted murder figures for 2004/5 then they were likely to be between 1600 and 2300 and not the 828 actually recorded in the crime figures.

Of course, Scotland is not alone in suffering from violence, it is a worldwide problem. Every year millions of children suffer abuse and neglect at the hands of their parents and care givers. One in two female murder victims is killed by her male partner after, or during, an ongoing abusive relation - ship, and one in four women experiences sexual abuse by an intimate partner during her lifetime. Violence kills about 4,500 people around the world every single day. That amounts to over 1.6 million deaths from violence per annum – 54 per cent are suicides, 35 per cent are homicides and 11 per cent are victims of war.

Countries vary considerably from one another on their

levels of violence. Some have much worse rates than Scotland's and there is a danger that by comparing ourselves to these other countries we begin to think that we are not that bad. After all, in real numbers, we compare favourably with South Africa, Nicaragua and Colombia. But is this the measure of our aspirations?

At that time Glasgow had the highest rate of murder in Europe per head of population. What's more, the rate of murder committed with a knife was three and a half times higher than that of England and Wales. The 2002 WHO report on violence highlighted Scotland as having a homicide rate for males aged between 10–29 of 5.3 per 100,000 population, the overall rate being 3.1. This rate is similar to Argentina, Costa Rica and Lithuania. The rate in England and Wales for the same age group was at that time 1.0 per 100,000 – significantly lower.

So in a nutshell what we found is that violence in Scotland at that time was a chronic problem and that it had changed very little over the last thirty years. Indeed it had most likely been the same since the 1930s. We also confirmed that the Strathclyde Police Force area had the largest numbers of murders in Scotland. However, no area of the country was immune.

As I said in the previous chapter, murders were just the tip of the iceberg; underneath lay an increasing volume of attempted murders, serious and simple assaults and a culture of knife carrying. This was true despite concerted efforts by the police during repeated high profile enforcement opera-tions. The level of under-recording of violence makes any rise or fall in recorded violence a poor measure of success or failure. Indeed this means that communities experiencing violence on their streets, and sometimes in their homes, have a far more accurate understanding of violence levels, and these are often at odds with 'reported' levels. When senior police make something of the small percentage drops in violence they suggest that the media's reporting of violence is out of sync with reality. They also deliberately or unwittingly suggest that those communities who see or experience violence everyday are somehow out of step with what the crime statistics are telling us. But the truth is that, then as now, it is the police's perception of violence that tends to be wrong, not the public's.

Two questions: why and what works?

The second element of the WHO model that we were now enthusiastically embracing involved understanding why violence occurs. To answer this we needed a clearer picture of violence which allowed us to understand it better. If we could understand what factors make violence more likely to occur then it would be easier to develop and apply appropriate interventions that reduce the risk of violence thereby increasing protection from violence.

This then led us to the third element of the model. We knew we needed to find interventions that worked and we realised too that police or criminal justice agencies do not deliver many of the interventions that can help prevent violence. We hoped that a better understanding of the causes of violence would help us to identify those agencies which were best placed to intervene and prevent violence occurring.

Societies around the world all have an agreed set of standards or rules. The most basic of these rules include injunctions such as 'do not steal' and 'do not kill'. Of course there is an 'or else' sanction built into these rules. If you break a rule there is a punishment, prison currently being the most popular sanction. Prison as a sanction is a legitimate intervention but it is only partially successful in preventing violence; it works only while the offender is in prison, and not always even then.

This criminal justice model of dealing with crime is particularly ineffective as a response to violence. Despite the evidence to the contrary, countries around the world, including Scotland, have nonetheless persisted with this model. We make something illegal, we outline the sanction for committing the illegal act, we detect those who offend against the act and we send them to prison for a set time as punishment.

This model makes sense as a last resort, but over time it has become not only the response of first resort but also it is the most likely societal response to violence. Nations' confidence in this system is absolute with some even believing that punishment's deterrent effect is sufficient to prevent all crime, including violence. Indeed the common view is that the more severe the punishment sanction the greater the 'prevention' effect. However, if this were true the United States of America, which locks up a large proportion of its citizens, would be the safest place on the planet. It is not.

Imagine for a moment tackling health challenges in the same way as we now deal with violence. Let's imagine we had used this model to tackle tuberculosis. We would wait until the patient reported his/her infection to the doctor who would then commit them to a sanatorium with others with the same infection. We would do nothing with them, or for them, while they were in the sanatorium and if they got well they would get out and if they didn't then we wouldn't care anyway. If they got out we would put them straight back into the same environment where the infection was rife. Now this seems stupid and doesn't make sense, yet this is exactly what we do with young violent men whom we expect to become 'cured' of their violence. But the process makes no sense: we detect them, they go to prison, they get out of prison, they commit another act of violence, we detect them, they go to prison and so on *ad infinitum*.

Anti-social behaviour legislation is a recent example of our collective belief in this criminal justice model. Evidence to date suggests that making it illegal has not resolved the issue of anti-social behaviour.

During this research period we confirmed that there was evidence that many of the factors affecting violence were ones over which the police had no control. We began to think in terms of primary prevention, secondary prevention, tertiary prevention, reducing the risk and increasing protection. We used words like 'diagnosis', 'infection' and 'treatment' and a host of other words and phrases associated with health. Indeed when speaking about violence all our analogies quickly became medical. We even spoke about the role of the police as 'stabilizing the patient' and of violent men 'infecting' others with their violence.

Looking for the light

We kept Willie Rae up to date with our progress and he maintained an active interest in what we were doing. In these early days of our journey it was not unusual to get a call from his PA asking Karyn or myself to go and see him or to get a telephone call from him direct.

When we told him about the levels of under-reporting we thought he might be reluctant to let us say this out loud let alone publicly. He was not. He was surprisingly relaxed and told us instead to 'flush the numbers out'. He also allowed us the time to research and explore why the levels of violence were so high in Strathclyde. He did not just give us permission but positively encouraged us to think about violence in an entirely new way. He also provided contact detail for some key people. These included Alan Sinclair from Scottish Enterprise and Dr Harry Burns, then Director of Public Health at Glasgow Health Board.

We were invited to Bute House in Edinburgh to give a presentation on our work to the Scottish Cabinet. At the time Jack McConnell was the First Minister and Cathy Jamieson Justice Minister. We were allocated twenty minutes on the agenda.

We outlined what we had learned about public health and the need for better collaboration. We also explained that while the violence figures looked bad they were actually much worse given the levels of under recording. In the end we were there for over an hour, answering questions and discussing what we might do to make it better. It was a very good meeting and we were buoyed by their reaction to what we had to say. The civil servants who had arranged the meeting were also present and they were equally supportive of our work although, as civil servants, they did not actually display any outward signs of enthusiasm, just an occasional smile and a nod.

No doubt this successful meeting was one reason why in 2006 the Scottish Government gave the VRU a Scotland wide remit for violence reduction and provided funding for projects and some staff.

Our initial meetings with colleagues from other agencies had confirmed that before we could fully engage with them we first had to ensure that we, the police, were being as effective as we could be. We had to get on to the moral high ground and demonstrate our premise that no matter how effective the police are they cannot bring about sustained reductions in violence on their own.

One of the accepted policing practices of the time was known as 'high visibility' policing. This was based on the idea that the public were reassured when they could see police on the streets. Likewise criminals were deterred and crime prevented by more cops on the street. I'm not sure of the science behind this theory but it was certainly a feature of policing in Strathclyde at the time.

K markers

In 2004 Karyn established a method of 'process mapping' which focused on knife possession. Everyone who is detected for a crime is given a unique number and this number allows that person and that case to be tracked through the criminal justice process from detection to court and sentencing. By tracking everyone who was caught in possession of a knife we could better understand the process, including the time taken to report the case, the time taken to get to court; and the disposal, including sentence.

A police administrator placed a 'K' marker beside the name of everyone caught in possession of a knife and the VRU received copies of the relevant forms. This allowed us to track exactly what had happened in every case. Bearing in mind that at this time we had proportionately three and a half times the number of murders with a knife than England and Wales, this was a lot of work.

The policy of high visibility policing required officers to stay on the street and on patrol with only minimum time spent away from their beat. This meant that if officers stopped someone in the street carrying a knife they would not necessarily arrest him and take him to a police office as this would mean they would be off the street. In such circumstances officers would only arrest if the person was wanted on warrant or was on bail for a similar offence, or if the police believed he would commit a similar offence later, or they could not identify him.

The K marker survey established that it could take up to 14 months before someone caught in possession of a knife appeared at court. In the interim this person usually collected a series of other pending cases. In short we were allowing a drama to become a crisis.

We were also able to track how long it took for the officers to actually write their report and submit it to the Procurator Fiscal or PF. If the PF took no proceedings we would obtain a copy of the case and try to find out why. For example, if the issue was lack of understanding of the legislation we could suggest training for the officers. We produced a small pocket guide detailing the legislation in relation to knives, the relevant Acts and the police powers. If there was no apparent reason why proceedings were not being taken we could, very politely, ask the PF why. We could also ascertain the average sentence.

Knife related violence was a serious issue for Scotland and for Strathclyde in particular. We met with senior fiscals and together we agreed that we would focus our efforts on knife crime. Cath Dyer was the Procurator Fiscal at Glasgow and we had a great relationship with her. She was an excellent supporter in our early days, offering advice and crucially helping us gain access to Sheriffs and the Lord Advocate through the Crown Office. She was committed and pragmatic and fully supportive of what we were trying to do.

The Lord Advocate produces guidance in relation to the police exercising their power of arrest and he changed the guidelines for knife possession. The change meant that if someone was found to be in possession of a knife he was arrested and kept in custody until the first lawful day at court. The knife carrier was also fingerprinted, photographed and had samples of DNA taken. When the offender appeared at court the PF would either oppose bail or ask for the court to impose restrictions. These might include a curfew, such as staying at home between certain hours, or staying away from particular areas, like the city centre.

In order to assist the PF oppose bail we developed an 'enhanced antecedent' report. This included not only the personal circumstances of the accused but statistical evidence about the area of their home address. It included the number of gang fights that had occurred in that area in the previous month as well as the level of crime and violence in the area. This additional information allowed the PF to make a better case to the Sheriff about opposing bail or asking for particular bail conditions.

Our tactic was to raise the issue of violence, and particularly knife related violence, and make it a problem for everyone and not just the police and we started to describe violence as a 'shared agenda'.

We were also gaining a clearer idea of what out strategy might be using the public health model. We needed to have effective enforcement practice. That meant better coordination between the police and other criminal justice partners like local authorities, courts and prisons. We were particularly encouraged by our experience of how we were now dealing with knife crime – specifically how the police were now working closely with prosecutors and courts. The Fiscals were very good partners and immediately understood the shared agenda. We described this part of the emerging strategy as *contain and manage*.

At the same time we recognised the need for a collective approach to violence that placed the notion of prevention at its core.

A public health approach to violence

As we saw earlier, traditionally prevention in policing or criminal justice terms is mostly concerned with the physical security of property – alarms, barred windows, and trackers on cars. But for public health professionals, prevention is far more important. If we were to have any real and lasting impact on violence and reducing the number of victims, we needed to follow their example.

Public health describes prevention in terms of three categories, primary, secondary and tertiary. Primary is concerned with preventing violence before it occurs, secondary is about preventing any escalation of violent behaviour and tertiary concerns preventing violent offenders from re-offending. Of course, the prevention of violence is only made possible with a better understanding of all the causal factors of violence.

We were also becoming increasingly aware of the fundamental need to bring about attitudinal change in individuals and communities, as well as professionals and agencies. We had to be more collaborative, more focused on outcomes and more inclusive. We also had to make more use of science and research to do the right things.

Through introductions made by Sir Willie we met up with Alan Sinclair of Scottish Enterprise. Alan had set up a groundbreaking employment project in Glasgow called the Wise Group and then became Director of Skills at Scottish Enterprise. He was now a consultant.

Alan told about us about a survey he had carried out at Scottish Enterprise to identify the skills that were lacking in the workforce across Scotland. The results of this survey were not what Alan and his colleagues at Future Skills Scotland had anticipated. They had expected employers to identify lack of numeracy and literacy skills in the workforce as their biggest challenge. But they didn't. Employers reported the most significant skills which were often lacking in employees were, in order of importance: planning and organising; customer handling; problem solving; team working; and oral communication.

These are all 'non-cognitive' skills as they are the human attributes we all need to successfully negotiate life; make decisions about ourselves; establish and maintain relation - ships; and judge risk. Two big questions facing Alan and his team were 'how do people acquire these skills?' and what could they do to remedy this if Scotland's employers were right and people weren't acquiring these skills.

Alan then embarked on a programme of research and quickly discovered that these skills are formed in the early years of life, between 0–5. This was confirmed by what we already knew from George Hosking's report on the importance of the early years in the development of empathy.

Alan was particularly influenced by Professor James Heckman, an American economics professor and Nobel laureate who gave a lecture in Scotland in 2004. Heckman's longitudinal research showed the importance of a person's early years experience for their future development and trajectory in life. He concluded that the first few years in life were so important that for every pound spent on a child in the 0–5 age group, the state would have to spend seven pounds later in that person's life to achieve the same outcome. In other words, public investment was best made early in a child's life when it was likely to have most impact and therefore be cost effective. In practical terms this means spending money supporting parents and providing nursery provision and being less concerned about secondary schooling, and college or university education.

We too started to look at the research Alan was pouring over and were equally taken by Heckman's conclusions. Soon we could see that the policy we needed to develop to prevent violence was about the early years. Initially this was a surprise to us but it made immediate sense. I was also taken by a quote from Heckman concerning schools and education: 'A major determinant of successful schools is successful families. Schools can only work with what parents bring them.'

As we continued on our journey to understand better the causes of violence we found that there was a virtual mountain of evidence providing very plausible explanations for why violence occurs. There was also a plethora of evidenced based interventions and responses that could reduce, or even prevent, violence occurring. We were excited and we responded to each new piece of evidence we discovered like kids with new toys. I had taken to using the term *emerging evidence*, which simply meant that it was not necessarily new evidence but rather evidence that I had just found out about.

CHAPTER 3
Coalition building

We were beginning to make real strides in our under-standing of violence and in developing processes such as K markers to help us understand what was going on at the local level. But we also realised that we would not bring about a sustained reduction in violence unless other professional groups shared this understanding and commitment. Indeed we firmly believed that convincing everyone to change the way they did their business and to work in collaboration was going to be our biggest challenge.

Karyn and I set about meeting people from social work, health, education and police to tell them about what we were discovering about violence prevention. We presumed, as it turns out naïvely, that they too would be as excited as we were with the evidence and the possibilities it offered to reduce violence and make our reputation as a violent city and a violent country obsolete. It was at this point in our journey that we began to realise the drag effect that negative attitudes were having on progress.

Separate agendas

Wherever Karyn and I went we were always well received and no one was ever discourteous. They always listened intently as we outlined some of the data and evidence we had uncovered. I suspect now that what we were saying, and the way we were saying it, was not just disrespectful but even a little threatening. In effect, we were asserting that what we had all been doing up till now had not made a blind bit of difference to the levels of violence in Scotland, particularly in Glasgow. Everyone knows their own business best and so when a couple of people from the police show up and start telling professionals in other disciplines they needed to work in a different way, there was bound to be resistance.

From our perspective the problem was that public service agencies were each delivering their services to the same people, but with little or no attempt at co-ordination. Professionals were also defining individuals by the services they received. Health dealt with patients and victims; social work dealt with clients; police dealt with victims and offenders; and education dealt with pupils.

For example, after a gang fight, and there were lots of gang fights, those who were injured were labelled victims or patients and received victim services. Those the police caught were labelled offenders and received offender services. However, as we saw earlier, the reality is that which of the protagonists in a gang fight becomes a victim and which becomes an offender is usually random. Indeed the roles of victim and offender are often interchangeable. In education terms these victims or offenders are usually labelled as pupils, but at that time they were usually 'excluded' pupils. In short, the services were dealing with the same people but did not act as if they were.

So this is why, despite the rhetoric, we could see very few meaningful collaborations or co-ordination of services.

In 2004 Karyn and I gave a presentation to the executive committee of a local authority. This group included the directors from all the service departments including education, social work, leisure, libraries and so forth. In our presentation we outlined the challenge of knives and spoke about the need for everyone to become involved in reducing and preventing violence. At the end of the forty minute presentation, the Director of Education agreed that some of the pupils attending his schools did carry knives but he asserted that they did not bring them into the building. He suggested that they often hid their knives outside the school and recovered them when they left. This reasoning led him to conclude that knives were not a matter for the school, the teachers or education.

Karyn and I were a little shocked. She had been working on a 'death stare' which she deployed at that moment. Luckily it was not quite perfected. We were greatly encouraged by the fact that there were other directors at the meeting who looked appropriately shocked by the education director's response. Unlike him, they saw the connections, and the shared benefits, and offered to assist in any way they could.

We had a similar experience presenting at the Scottish Prison Service when a senior researcher there suggested the challenge was too big and that we should save ourselves the time and effort and 'no bother trying'. He too was very much in the minority among his colleagues.

However, complacency was all too common. We began to hear remarkably similar responses from the professionals we encountered, no matter what their profession. Phrases like 'we're already doing that' or 'we've tried that before and it doesn't work' or 'that's not really an issue for us' were fired at us constantly.

It was around this time that we began using a quote from Machiavelli's *The Prince*:

'There is nothing more difficult to carry out, nor more doubtful of success, nor more dangerous to conduct than to initiate a new order of things. For the reformer has enemies in all who profit by the old order and only lukewarm defenders in all those who profit by the new order.'

All public service organisations, agencies and services seem to have become bound to working practices, policies and strategies that can often restrict their effectiveness. Public services today seem to be founded on the same principles as commercial business organisations where value is only ever defined by monetary cost. It was therefore no surprise that the universal response to our presentations, at lots of different meetings, was 'have you got a budget?' There was certainly no shortage of suggestions and ideas as to how we might spend any budget we had. It appeared that resources were the only thing stopping everyone doing much better and solving society's problems. The answer to most challenges was apparently money; something that we had obviously missed.

If we always do what we've always done . . .

Our experiences were confirming the need for attitudinal

change if we were to progress. Neither Karyn nor I had previously been involved in the business of prevention or community safety and so we came at the problem from the position of enthusiastic amateurs. We had discovered evidence of a new way of undertaking prevention work that had the potential to make a real difference and we were excited by the opportunity. We thought too that violence prevention would be a unifying subject: who does not want to reduce or prevent violence? What's more we thought people would do the right thing simply because it was the right thing to do. Looking back I can see that we were incredibly naïve and happily oblivious to the obstacles, some real but sometimes illusionary, in the way of progress.

We were, from the outset, convinced that collaborations and partnerships would be the only way to achieve sustainable reductions in violence.

Successive governments had realised the need for effective partnership working and the need to do things in a different way and they had established local Community Planning Partnerships and Community Safety Partnerships to coordinate local services better. It seemed to us at the time, however, that the prevailing notion of an effective partner - ship was not really about delivering positive outcomes or real collaboration. No, the definition of a successful partnership was working together to make each partner's job easier or to make joint bids for more funding. Many of the new practices did not seem to be aimed at effectiveness or even efficiency and very few had built in sustainability.

The fact that there was already a framework for partnership working meant that when we started to speak with people from other agencies including social work, education and prisons many told us that the partnerships and collaborations we were suggesting as a new way of working were already in place and happening. When we paid closer attention we discovered that there were indeed lots of strategies, policies, projects and initiatives. However, as far as we could see, they were not penetrating the permafrost of middle management and delivering their promise.

It became obvious that if we were to start doing things differently we would first need to convince, cajole and coax everyone, particularly professionals, to change how they thought as well as how they operated. A real change in attitudes was required before we could even begin to tackle violence effectively and make any headway.

We began to develop the idea of a *shared agenda* supported by reasoned argument and well founded evidence. We defined the issue of violence as an issue for everyone and not just criminal justice. This was the reason we were called the Violence Reduction Unit and not the Violent *Crime* Reduction Unit. We thought that if crime were in the title then everyone would presume it was a problem just for the police. On reflection this was a very smart insight.

By this time the Scottish Government had also realised that the silo working mentality of many in the public sector was limiting ambitions and frustrating aspiration across subject areas. They realised too that continuing to do more of the same would not have the impact they wanted. As a consequence they had structured much of their funding and grant making arrangements to favour partnership working and innovation. Many of the agencies and local authority departments had become very well versed in sourcing funding, especially from government. They knew how to frame funding bids in ways that fulfilled the government criteria for getting the money.

There were unintended consequences for this policy – consequences that did not do much to make real the genuine desire for more collaborative working. Neither did it help increase effective practice and delivery.

Bids for funding were weighted in favour of those that involved more than one agency working on the project and also on new ideas or strategies that had not been tried before. This was presumably why any time we suggested doing something differently to improve services or delivery we kept being asked 'do you have a budget?' Indeed it seemed to us that for some the measure of an effective leader was how much funding they could source from government.

Even though bids were jointly submitted by more than one organisation, essentially there was seldom any real change to practice, delivery or outcomes. Perhaps because little real change was coming out of partnership working, the Scottish Government and various agencies came to value innovation over effectiveness. Thus it became more important to assert that it was a new idea rather than claim it was an effective idea. So in assessing a project, 'has this been done before?' became a vitally important question.

Very few projects were ever conducted on a sizeable scale. There were literally hundreds of pilot schemes. As most were never evaluated they were never deemed to have failed. Even if they were judged a huge success, when the government funding ended, the pilot stopped as they were inevitably short term. All of this was hugely frustrating for many recipients of services.

The reason usually given for such pilots ending was simply that the money had run out. There appeared to be very little co-ordination of national policy or strategy and it created service delivery that was short term, transient and usually very ineffective. It was also very frustrating for many front line professionals from every agency. There were some who were intent on fixing the blame and not fixing the problem but we also discovered many who were ready to change and do things differently. We wanted to change the way we did our work as individual agencies but more importantly we wanted to change how we worked together to deliver better outcomes – the shared agenda. We knew more of the same was not an option if we wanted to make things better, particularly in relation to violence prevention.

Finding allies

We soon began to put the professionals we met into three distinct groups. Those who saw the light; those who were startled by the light; and those who were in the dark.

We began to identify a 'coalition of the willing' comprising key people in local authorities who understood why we wanted to change the way we did our business. These were not always the strategic leaders or directors. Some were, like us, senior managers who were close enough to the point of impact to understand that we all had do something different.

We were now realising that if we wanted to fundamentally change the way we delivered services we would have to find ways to influence outwith our authority. In effect we would have to move from a culture of command and *control* to more of a culture of command and *convince*.

Partnership working is very difficult and consumes lots of energy; we knew this. Investigating a murder is relatively straightforward as there is a single goal, a professional team and a leader. Similarly, an A&E doctor dealing with an injured casualty has a single goal, a professional team and a leader. Now trying to get these two teams to work together on a shared goal is not easy. What is the shared goal? Who is the leader? What's more, the professional language, standards and norms are all different. This is why we did not under - estimate the scale of our task. It also led us to question the status quo: if we require several different agencies to deliver a single outcome then perhaps the agencies themselves are wrongly set up.

Revolution was not the plan, at least not then. But we became more revolutionary when we started to broaden our thinking on territorialism and gangs and the corrosive impact this was having on progress. As we started to look at the territorial youth gangs in Glasgow we noted a remarkable and surprising similarity between their behaviour and the behaviour of the professional 'gangs' we were trying to engage with. The professional or agency gangs were territorial and resolutely protected their turf. Many were aloof and displayed a conceit about the importance and uniqueness of their role that often led to arrogance. They often failed to, or refused to, recognise and acknowledge the shared agenda and the influence and impact their work had on other agencies.

In organisations it is now commonplace to talk about 'failure demand', which refers to something not done at an early stage of a process which later produces a negative impact. In relation to our shared public service agenda on violence we were finding that failure demand concerned the failures of one agency impacting on the demands and performance of other agencies. We realised that what we needed was a clearer sense of the shared agenda and a shared outcome.

I think that Karyn and I are both very persuasive and we began to establish a network of like-minded individuals from different agencies and professions. We would meet people individually and discuss with them what we were trying to do. In effect we were creating a *coalition of the willing*. It was not that difficult to do because many were, like us, becoming frustrated with doing the same things and getting the same outcomes.

We knew too that we needed to let as many people as possible know what we were doing and what we were hoping to achieve. This meant engaging with the media, politicians, professional groups, communities – in fact we would speak to any group, anywhere, anytime. We put ourselves about and made ourselves available. We wrote to every MSP and MP in Strathclyde and invited them individually into the VRU. Many accepted our invitation and when they visited we presented them with evidence and told them about our ideas to reduce and prevent violence.

We also invited editors of newspapers into the office and told them a similar story. We asked them if, when covering violent incidents, including murder, they would give the wider perspective on what we were doing. We let them know that we didn't want cheerleaders. Nonetheless we let them know that they had a significant role to play in informing the public about our new way of working. Most got it, some didn't get it and some got it but ignored it.

In the main the Scottish media have been excellent supporters of our work. For our part we told it as it was. We followed Willie Rae's advice and put reported crime figures in context and tried to flush out the real levels of violence. Inevitably this meant that we didn't get many invites to tourist office parties and some professionals, including senior police personnel, told us we were wrong, claiming that the Scotland we described was not recognisable to the vast majority of Scots. They are partly correct but for many Scots violence is an everyday part of normal life.

CHAPTER 4

David's story

In 2007 we were asked to present to the Scottish Govern-
ment's 'Equally Well' group which had been formed to
improve the general well-being of Scots but particularly tackle
the disparity of health outcomes between affluent and poor
areas. Harry Burns, our ally, was the Chief Medical Officer
and a member of this group. In his first annual report as CMO
on the health of the nation, he included a chapter on violence
which Karyn had written. This was the first time anywhere
that a Chief Medical Officer's report included a chapter on
violence.

Presenting to the Equally Well group was a real opportunity
for us to influence opinions and national policy development
so we spent a lot of time shaping the presentation. By this
time we had delivered countless presentations to numerous
audiences about violence prevention and we had usually
included a piece of CCTV footage. This showed a gang fight
and a passer-by being stabbed. The man subsequently died
from the single stab wound. His murderer was arrested. We
decided that the best way to make an impact on the Equally
Well Group and change attitudes towards violence was to
craft a message about how prevention was more effective,

more efficient and better all round than the current approach. We knew that we needed to personalise the message as much as possible. Karyn set about creating a narrative about David, the young boy in the CCTV footage who had inflicted the fatal stab wound. The presentation was entitled 'David's Story – Born to Fail'. It soon became the corner stone of our argument for earlier and more effective intervention and primary prevention.

It is difficult to quantify exactly how many times we have told the story or how many people have seen it. But I reckon that it is tens of thousands. We have also told the story and delivered the presentation in several countries and the message is always understood; its impact is always powerful.

The circumstances

At the time of the murder David lived in the 14th most deprived ward in Scotland. There were loads of gangs in the area, all territorial and all engaging in recreational violence often involving weapons like knives, golf clubs, bricks, bottles or whatever was handy. David was involved with these gangs.

One night, aged fifteen, David was in Glasgow city centre with some other members of his gang. A fight started with a gang from another area. David had a knife with him. He had used it earlier that same night to rob someone of his baseball cap. During the fight David stabbed a man once in the upper torso. His victim was not a member of a rival gang, not another violent young man, but a wholly innocent passer by who had been walking up Buchanan Street at the time of the fight. He died at the scene.

David did not leave home that night to murder anyone. When he was at school his ambition was not be a murderer.

It is true that David was carrying a knife. He always carried a knife and most of his friends carried a knife. He had stabbed people before and they hadn't died. He had been stabbed before and hadn't died and he knew lots of people who had been stabbed and hadn't died. He was fighting in a gang. This was what he'd always done. It's what his friends did. David was conforming to his environment and perhaps he was even conforming to expectations.

David was arrested and convicted of culpable homicide and sentenced to seven years in prison. Unlike many stabbings when it can be difficult to distinguish between offender and victim, in this instance it is easy to see who is responsible and it is clear who to blame. David had the knife. It was David who stabbed. It was David who lived.

We are all very comfortable with this clear and unambiguous apportioning of blame. It allows the media to say David is a Vicious Thug, A Hooligan, A Yob, A Ned, Scum, Feral. According to the press he represents a growing trend whereby young people are out of control and have no respect. Needless to say I have no respect for such a view of young people.

It's always reassuring to know exactly who is to blame particularly if each of us can say that we had no personal responsibility: if we can convince ourselves that it was the fault of *others*, the responsibility of others and that only *others* were involved.

This murder was not a difficult enquiry for the investigators. We had CCTV footage of the incident. We had DNA. We had witnesses. We had David.

In using David's story we were able to demonstrate the connections between agencies and the impact and conse - quence of these connections. In 2007 it cost about £34,000 to keep someone in prison for a year. David got seven years so that's £238,000. If we take into account the costs of the police enquiry, the trial costs and the future burden David's life will put on public funds we can very quickly demonstrate the economic case for prevention. Public policy is usually founded on cost but sadly this prevention equation seems to have had little effect on Criminal Justice policy.

If our response to cases of violence like David's is to pass more punitive laws we'll need more police, courts, prisons and lawyers. We will of course in all likelihood also have more victims. Prevention makes economic sense.

A murder waiting to happen?

So how did David, aged fifteen, become a murderer? In the presentation we tell David's story from birth. He was born in 1981. His mum was an alcoholic and lived on income support. He has a big sister. At that point they lived in the 19th most deprived ward in Scotland.

In 1984 he moved with his mum to the 17th most deprived ward in Scotland. They moved because his father was abusing his mother physically. In 1985 David and his mum moved to the 9th most deprived ward in Scotland because of continuing harassment from his mum's ex partner, his dad.

In 1988 they moved again, this time back to the 19th most deprived ward in Scotland. By this time David is seven years old.

In 1989 when he was eight years old David's mother could not cope so he moved in with his maternal grandmother through the week. She also lives in the 19th most deprived ward.

Living in his grandmother's house at that time were three adult uncles who had about 120 previous convictions between them, mostly for drugs, violence and dishonesty. Social Work placed David into this environment because they considered it to be better than where he was living with his mum and in comparison it probably was.

In 1990 the family were re-housed again due to ongoing harassment from the ex partner. During the period between 1990 and 1993 the family moved home a further three times due to local authority plans for demolition and regeneration. In 1993 they were living in the 14th most deprived ward in Scotland.

All this time David had been attending school. In 1993 he started secondary school. His head teacher remembers him and describes him as diminutive in stature in comparison with other boys in his year.

He started truanting at eleven and two years later he was doing so regularly. By the time he was thirteen he had been charged twice with breach of the peace, and was referred to the Children's Panel. He was considered 'outwith parental control' and social work became involved.

The Children's Panel system was created in Scotland to deal with children at risk. Its fundamental principle is to deal with the need and not the deed. It is an excellent system but I believe it's often overwhelmed with the volume of cases it has to deal with every day.

By the time David reached fourteen he had been charged with housebreaking, assault, shoplifting and theft. This is the same year that the family moved to a house back in the 19th most deprived ward in Scotland where they stayed for a year before moving to another house in the same area. David was described at this time as 'classroom disruptive'. He was using alcohol and abusing solvents and he was excluded from school intermittently.

David was also made the subject of a Home Supervision order. The family was very resistant to social work involvement and his grandmother was very practised at dealing with services. In 1996 he was charged with the theft of cars. In 1997, aged fifteen, he was charged with assault, assault and robbery, attempted murder and, as we know, murder. He was found guilty of culpable homicide and sentenced to seven years. In his post trial report the trial judge said:

> There did not seem to be any indication in the
> background or supporting evidence suggesting that
> David is anything other than a pretty ordinary
> teenager, although one familiar with general gang
> culture, involving significant and indeed quite
> organised violence between different territorial
> groups. He seems to have a decent and supportive
> family and to feel genuine abhorrence for what he did.

David's life cannot ever be considered ordinary. The judge's comments will have been based on a social enquiry report and, in relation to the caseload of the social worker who prepared the report perhaps David's life was pretty ordinary. I worked in that area and I can understand how it would seem so.

In 2002, when David was nineteen and still in prison, his

mum died of a heroin overdose and his sister was in secure accommodation.

David was allowed escorted leave from prison in 2003 and was caught with two other prisoners dealing drugs. In 2004 David was released on licence back into the same house, in the same street, where he had lived when he had committed the murder. When he was released this is what is noted in the release report: 'Scottish Ministers note that on release David can look forward to strong support from his grandmother and his wider family in Glasgow and his employment prospects look favourable.'

In a rather perverse way David's employment prospects were favourable: a young man with a conviction for murder, lacking empathy, comfortable using violence, and with a local reputation, will not readily get a job through the Job Centre, but there will be plenty of 'work' for him near his home. It would be comforting to think that David might stay at home and not frighten anyone. It would also be reassuring to think that he will have learned his lesson. But it would be incredibly naïve to believe either.

David is now a dad; his son was born in 2007. They live in the same street. David was never parented and as a result I am not sure he will be able to father his own son effectively. I am not talking about whether he becomes a bad parent or a good parent simply a 'good enough parent' and the best parent he can be.

The lessons

Sadly David's story is not unique. It is true that not every violent event ends in murder but that is what always grabs the attention. The truth is that the outcome is largely a happenstance. That's why we must concentrate our efforts on addressing the behaviour and not just focus on dealing with the outcome after the violent crime has been committed.

David is difficult to like, but we have to remember that he and his mother needed support before he was even born, and they didn't get it. As a society we only began to pay attention to David when he started to annoy us; when he started to commit crime; when he started to be a nuisance. We missed those teachable moments where perhaps a positive intervention would have helped him and his mum.

There are far too many Davids out there – not easy to like, hard to love. But he was a child when he murdered and the adults in his life who should have protected him and nurtured him didn't. His mum couldn't do it because she was an alcoholic living with an abusive man; she could not even look after herself.

It's all too easy to forget about the Davids. Maybe it's because they are difficult, troubled and troublesome. It's not easy to empathise with David the murderer, but David's behaviour is a consequence of his life, particularly his early life. He needed help when he was the victim of violence and neglect, when his mother was the victim of violence from his dad. But we didn't help David the baby or David the child so it's hardly surprising that we don't help David the murderer. But what about David the dad?

During the investigation of a murder we call the first few hours of the enquiry the 'golden hours'. That's when vital decisions are made and if they are not made then it might be too late and the opportunity to get evidence will be lost. For example, we need to allow forensic teams to recover evidence. If we do not, evidence will be lost and never recovered. I think the early years of life are the golden years and enriching children's lives during these early years and helping parents and caregivers be as good as they can be makes a fabulous difference.

So by presenting David's story, Karyn and I were able to point to the various points in his life when we could have done something that may have helped prevent a murder. The story makes sense to everyone who has heard it. It made sense to the Equally Well group who went on to establish the early Years Task Force and the Early Years Collaborative which aim to improve the early years experience for every child in Scotland.

David's story helped all this happen and I am minded to seek out David and tell him.

CHAPTER 5

The Glasgow gangs

David was only one of legions of boys involved in youth gangs in Glasgow. Gangs were a particular problem for the city and had been so for decades. Agency responses to the gangs had remained largely unaltered over the years. Violence was an issue throughout Scotland but Glasgow had a particular problem with knife related violence and youth gangs. We realised that if we were to have any impact on violence reduction we had to take on this most challenging issue. This was part of our unwritten strategy to get policing onto the moral high ground. After all who could object to trying to eradicate youth violence and making our communities safer.

In 2007 we tasked each of the eight territorial police divisions in Strathclyde to produce a profile of the gangs in their area. This was carried out by divisional intelligence analysts. The results confirmed that particular geographical areas had persistently high levels of gang related violence. The east end of Glasgow stood out as it had the biggest problem both in terms of the number of gangs and the level of gang violence.

The Greater Easterhouse profile showed that there were

55 known gangs containing over 600 members between them. These were young white men ranging in age from 9 to early 20s with the peak age for involvement between 14 and 18.

These young men were obsessed by respect, were highly territorialised and appeared to be resistant to change. So if we could do something about the gangs and levels of violence in the east end of Glasgow then we could do something about these challenges everywhere.

It is important to realise that there is a difference between these youth gangs and organised criminal gangs. We liked to term the violence that the youth gangs were involved in as 'recreational' – it's what they did. It was about territory certainly but it was not about organised criminality. These gangs were not defending 'drug turf ' or criminal extortion. They were fighting because there was a tradition of gangs in their neighbourhood. Some of these young men did end up involved with organised crime gangs and their lack of empathy, violent disposition and reputation served them well in this new role. Nonetheless this is not how they got into violence.

We wanted to have a clear and contemporary picture of the Greater Easterhouse area. Up until then the Police and others had relied solely on crime statistics but we wanted to create a richer and more complete profile of the area. We found data about the area from other sources and this too helped define the shared agenda, who would be our partners and who was best placed to help. Here's some of what we discovered:

> There was a resident population of just over 60,000 with 27 per cent of the residents under 20 years of

age. The number of adults without any qualifications was 49 per cent above the national average and the number with five or more standard grade passes was 14 per cent below the national average. The number of wholly workless households was 122 per cent above the national average and the number of income-deprived people was 114 per cent.

When it came to crime, serious violent crime was 170 per cent above the national average and domestic abuse, vandalism and drug offending all exceeded the national averages by 54 per cent, 22 per cent and 39 per cent respectively.

Having defined the problem now we had to do something about it. But we still did not have a specific plan. We knew policing on its own would not sort the problem. We were committed to the public health model and this helped us define the notion of a shared agenda and identify partners.

Off the shelf intervention

Early in 2007 Karyn attended a conference in the United States. It was a conference of Chief Police Officers, predominantly from the US but with a few invited European chiefs too. Sir Willie was one of the invited chiefs from the UK and he nominated Karyn as his representative.

While she was there she met with Professor David Kennedy who had been working with gangs in Boston where he introduced a 'focused deterrence' model. This had been proving so successful in reducing violence that the press were calling it 'the Boston Miracle'. Kennedy also introduced the same approach in Cincinnati. Karyn returned excited about

Kennedy's ideas and what they had achieved. His model had been proven to work, albeit in a city in the United States, and she believed it could also work in Glasgow.

The model is very straightforward and involves three elements. First authorities tell the gangs that the community has had enough and that the fighting must stop and if it doesn't the police and others will come down very hard on gang members. If they stopped fighting then various organisations would work hard to find other things for them to do.

In technical language these three elements could be summarised as follows:

- Enforcement – stop fighting or else
- The moral voice of the community – we have all had enough so stop
- Services – finding diversions, interventions and alternatives for gang members.

We had always been at great pains to keep things simple and we loved the simplicity of Kennedy's model. In the past we had found that most plans and strategies were so complex and complicated that they only made sense to the authors. They seldom delivered anything tangible and yet they continued to be produced.

One of Kennedy's programmes in the United States was called 'the Cincinnati Initiative to Reduce Violence'or CIRV (pronounced serve). It was largely driven by church leaders, mainly from the Baptist church. It also spoke with the 'voice of the community'. There was also a very hard line policing policy in that state, supported by a very robust and rigid approach to prosecution. This 'three strikes and you're out' policy made the 'or else' part of the model very easy to apply. We did not have these same advantages in Glasgow.

In Scotland we had seen improvements in legislation, the length of sentence for knife carrying increased and the Lord Advocate's guidelines enhanced.

We were particularly weak, however, when it came to the 'moral voice' of our communities. This had initially surprised us. We had thought people would be outraged when a local victim was murdered but they were not. There would usually be a temporary street 'shrine' created by the victim's friends but this never translated into the sort of outrage that resulted in change. Our communities seemed to accept that there was nothing that could be done about the gangs or violence. They appeared to accept it all as normal. What we found even more alarming was that this view seemed to be shared by many of the public, and voluntary agencies that worked in those communities.

In 2007 Karyn and I had been invited to attend a round table meeting at the Home Office in London convened by the then Home Secretary John Reid. This meeting was organised in response to three separate murders that had occurred in London over a single weekend. The communities there had demanded that something be done about the violence and the activities of youth gangs. We'd had similarly awful weekends in Glasgow when young men in their teens had lost their lives in separate incidents but there was no community outrage, no banging on the doors of politicians, no demand that the violence should stop.

In the early days of the VRU we had harboured a hope that

there might be 'a Rosa Parks moment' in Glasgow – a moment following an incident, a murder, when we would all come together and say we've had enough. That moment never came.

What we did have in Glasgow, that was better than the US, was a more robust and comprehensive structure of statutory and other support services that were already being delivered in the east end. We were certain too that we could mobilise a good policing response. We were confident that we could prioritise, focus and co-ordinate existing services on the young men engaged in gangs and gang violence. We wanted to keep it simple: all we wanted to do was reduce gang related violence and we were convinced that the focused deterrence model that had worked in Boston, and was beginning to see results in Cincinnati, would work for the gangs in Glasgow.

Managing the process

Our first job was to convince Willie Rae and the Force Executive that we should do this. We recognised the risk to the reputation of the force if, in effect, we 'threatened' to do something that we could not deliver. Imagine the risk involved in telling a community quite specifically that we're going to sort out their gang problem and then we failed to do so.

We presented our plan to the Force Executive in 2007 and they agreed without hesitation. That meant we had one of three elements in place – enforcement.

Karyn and I then spent the next few months visiting partner agencies and meeting with people from social work, housing, education, the local community and third sector groups,

Scottish Government, local politicians, procurator fiscals, sheriffs, Career Scotland . . . in fact anyone connected to the east end and who could help with our plan.

We did not make any public announcements. Instead we spoke individually with the people we thought would be key to delivering the plan. We had met some of these people already on our journey and we were confident that we would at least get a hearing.

We encountered some real allies, dedicated people who saw immediately the potential of the initiative. People who were, like us, fed up doing the same old thing again and again. Of course we also met some negative types who believed the problem couldn't be fixed or made better and therefore it wasn't worth the effort. In short, folk who thought – why even try?

The individuals who joined us from the social work and education departments and Glasgow Housing Association were particularly enthusiastic and supportive. So too were the sheriffs at Glasgow Sheriff Court.

Sheriffs seem always to get a bad press about what they do and say. They are often referred to in the media as being out of touch and their position does not permit them to speak about their role. From the very first meeting with the Sheriff Principal and subsequent meetings with Glasgow sheriffs they were fully committed, supportive and encouraging in the entire CIRV initiative.

We also had outstanding support from the civil servants working in the Community Safety Unit in Edinburgh, another group who don't always get good press coverage.

We had recruited an experienced Detective Chief Inspector who had worked with the VRU before and whom we knew would have the right sort of skills to head up the initiative. He was resourceful, resilient and smart.

By summer 2008 we had identified all the key people in the different agencies and groups and secured their buy in to the CIRV initiative. We invited David Kennedy to Scotland and also Greg Baker the man who ran CIRV in Cincinnati. We organised meetings with all the key partners to make sure we cemented in their commitment and support. Kennedy and Baker also helped resolve the issues and doubts about the detail of the delivery as this is where 99 per cent of failures occur. We knew this initiative worked in the US but whether we could get it to work in Scotland was another matter.

We had kept our Scottish Government contacts fully apprised of our work and had also met with Justice Minister, Kenny MacAskill and Fergus Ewing who was responsible for Community Safety. While the mainstay of our plan was to try to co-ordinate existing services better, we also recognised the need for some extra funding to develop particular inter - ventions and Scottish Government were very supportive.

Kennedy and Baker were outstanding. They gave their time, experience and knowledge for free and we worked them hard while they were here. Kennedy in particular was not precious about his model and allowed us to adapt it to our Scottish context. In effect we knew this model was effective but we didn't know if we could deliver it in Scotland, so the test was of our ability and not of the model. Kennedy asked what our performance measures were going to be. In other words, how would we know if the initiative was really working. Again we had decided to keep it simple. All we wanted to know was 'has gang related violence reduced in the east end of Glasgow?'

We could have designed a whole suite of measures incorporating the full spectrum of our partners' interests – exclusions from school, hospital admissions, referrals to children's reporter, number of pupils leaving school to positive destinations, number of evictions, etc. Kennedy even suggested that we measure the number of gangs we get rid of, but we explained that it wasn't the gang that was the issue: it was what they did as a gang that was the problem.

The young men we were dealing with were violent in the gang, violent on their own and violent in pairs. Violence was the issue. People form groups everywhere. We are all in groups and organisations of one type or another. They can share some characteristics such as territorial protectiveness. We all need to be connected to one another and gangs do that. So trying to dismantle the gangs would be an impossible task and ultimately fruitless.

We set a date to start the initiative – October 2008. We knew that we were not fully prepared but we also knew that if we didn't set a tight date then we might never get it going. Karyn, in particular, was very keen to set a tight deadline. It worked.

We established a case management team with people from education, social work, police, community safety services, Children's Reporter, PF, Glasgow housing. It was this team's task to ensure that all the various services were co-ordinated and focused. This group too collated and exchanged information about the individual gangs. We realised that the sharing of information would be a vital component of focused activity. History indicated that it was in the area of information exchange that most joint initiatives had floundered. There is legislation in place that facilitates the exchange of personal information between agencies in particular circumstances and for particular outcomes. Reducing violence and increasing community safety were two of them.

The exchange and use of information is vital to any project. Our experience and understanding of partnership working and inter agency collaboration had taught us that it was usually a lack of information exchange that caused projects and plans to fail. We understood too that the effective exchange of information would depend on the personal relationships developed between the representatives from the different agencies involved in the project. This is particularly important in the effectiveness of the case management team who were at the heart of the whole project. Information is most likely to be exchanged between people who know and trust each other, where there is no rivalry and where the shared outcomes are agreed and clear to all involved. That's what we created with the CIRV case management team. It was the real engine room of CIRV as it was where all the key decisions were made and results delivered.

Glasgow Housing Association provided a 24-hour free phone number which dealt with calls from gang members. Any gang member who contacted this number would be referred to the case management team and they would assess each individual. They considered information from every source available, such as previous convictions, housing data, school report, police intelligence and any relevant facts which would help make the right decision and get the appropriate help.

The launch

In preparation for the launch of CIRV we had deliberately not told the gangs exactly what we were planning. But we used youth workers, community cops, housing officers, social workers, teachers to spread the message that something different was happening and that it would start sometime in October.

By then we knew who the gang members were and where they lived but we still had to find ways to reach them and convince them to engage with the diversion and inter - ventions we had planned for them and, of course, to stop fighting.

There was a specific element of the Cincinnati CIRV that was troubling me and it was largely about how we comm u - ni cated with the gang members. Cincinnati considered the way they handled this aspect of the process a vital element of the success. In the US projects the gang members were brought together with members of their community and their behaviour openly challenged. They were told of the damage they were doing to their communities and their families and themselves. The police confronted them and told then that they would be sent to prison if they didn't stop fighting and told them about other things that they could do instead. This all took place in a community church or community hall and was led by the local minister. They referred to this part of the process as a 'Call In'. It was likely to be cathartic and I worried that it would not work here in Scotland. I thought our Calvin genes would get in the way and undercut any emotion. Thankfully others in the team disagreed with me and argued their case. As a result we included the Call In as part of the

Scottish CIRV, although we changed the name to a 'Self Referral Session'.

Community cops, housing officers, youth workers, teachers, social workers, working in the area had been actively encouraging, persuading, convincing, and cajoling gang members to attend the first Self Referral Session which took place in October 2008. We believed that if this was to be powerful, real, life changing drama then we required a setting that portrayed the importance and seriousness of what we were doing. We chose the Glasgow Sheriff Court.

The day arrived and I felt very apprehensive. We had no idea if this whole thing would work but we had placed this event at the heart of the process and it was too late for second thoughts. I've been at court and given evidence on hundreds of occasions but that day I felt more nervous and more unsure than I'd ever felt on a court day. We had an invited audience of teachers, social workers, community workers, charities, academics and some of the people who had helped get the initiative to this stage. We had police on duty in and around the court and they were all in full uniform – stab vests, batons . . . These costumes were there to help drive home the 'or else' element.

Eighty-five gang members attended that first Referral Session. Different gangs were represented and they all sat together in the public area of the court. Some had been bussed in. Some came on their own. Some wanted to be there and some did not. The youngest was about sixteen and the oldest about twenty-two. Most were teenagers. Some looked defiant and some looked nervous, though not as nervous as me, or the team.

The cops stood among the gang members in the public area. The non gang members we had invited sat in the well of the court and around the sides, including the jury box. The dock was empty.

We had set up television screens around the court.

The Sheriff entered and walked to his seat and everyone in the court stood. The Sheriff was the first to speak. He thanked everyone for coming, reminding them that it was a court of law and that it was his court therefore his rules would apply. He pointed to the gang members at the rear of the court saying he was particularly pleased they had come because even if they did not care about themselves, other people cared about them. This simple, unscripted human message, delivered in the context of what we were trying to do, was electric and set the tone for the whole event.

Remember that the message we wanted to convey to the gang members was that everyone had had enough, there were alternatives and we would help them to do other things but above all the violence must stop.

The plan was that several people would speak to the gangs, each for no more than five minutes. Each speaker was assigned a particular part of message.

The first to address them after the Sheriff was a senior police officer. He told them that Strathclyde Police was a bigger gang than any they were in and that he would personally make sure that anyone involved in gang fighting would be caught. He said that tomorrow was a new day and that things were going to be very different because everyone was tired of the violence and the fighting. While he spoke the television screens showed pictures of the gang members, maps showing their gang areas and where they fought, charts showing who was in what gang. He said if one gang member stepped out of line then every gang member would be held to account.

As he talked he walked among the gang members and I could see some looking defiant. It was a look I recognised and had seen often enough. It was a look that said 'come on then, come ahead, I'm not scared of you'. It summed up in a single look the aggressive, thrawn nature of a type of young Scottish man.

After his allotted five minutes was up it was the turn of a maxillofacial surgeon who spoke about how difficult it is to repair some of the wounds inflicted during gang fights. He said his patients usually weren't that brave when they were on a hospital trolley waiting to be stitched or go to theatre. While he was talking the TV screens showed pictures of wounds inflicted by knives, machetes, bricks, and golf clubs. The gang members response to this talk was to look away from the screens.

The surgeon finished by showing pictures of babies with cleft pallets. He explained that, through no fault of their own, some babies are born like this. He told them he has the skill to fix these babies' deformities but they have to wait because he is too often working on gang members who have been injured during a fight. So these babies were suffering because of their fighting, their violence, and it had to stop. Some of them hung their heads.

Now a mum spoke. A mum whose son had been murdered. Her son was in a gang and carried a knife. He was seventeen when he was murdered, stabbed in the street and died before he even got to hospital. She told them how she sometimes forgets he is dead and texts him, or buys food to make his favourite dinner. How she can still smell him when she goes into his room. All their heads were down when she spoke and I suspect some were close to tears. I was. Her plea to them was not to do the same thing to their mums, to do good things with their lives and make their mothers proud.

They then heard from a mentor who had been in a gang, been in prison and done everything that they were involved in. He told them it was never too late to change. It was possible and there were people who would help; they just had to stop fighting and ask. He told a story about being at his mum's funeral with a prison officer because he was serving a sentence. He said it occurred to him there that throughout his life he had never sent his mum a birthday card or a mother's day card. He felt ashamed.

We then heard from a couple of men who ran youth football projects. They confirmed it was never too late to change and they were being given a great opportunity. All they had to do was call the number and they would help them change and be the best they could be.

Each of the gang members had been given a card when they entered the court, on which was a free phone number that would be staffed 24/7, if they wanted help. If they wanted to stop fighting then all they had to do was call this number. This was a small thing to do but a huge step to take for these young men and each of the speakers was urging them to take this first step.

Next up was an African American basketball player who played for Glasgow Rocks. He told them about his brother dying in his arms from gunshot wounds. He told them not to be afraid to change.

A church minister from Ruchazie told them about redemption, it was never too late and they had people who would help them. They just had to decide.

The last contribution was from Jack Black, an inspirational speaker who runs an organisation called Mind Store which promotes personal development. Jack had been a social worker in Easterhouse and when I called him to tell him what we were trying to do he immediately volunteered his services.

When Jack stood up he told them how he worked in Easterhouse twenty years earlier trying to divert young men like them from violence. He recounted the story of a young man he worked with during his time in Easterhouse. This young man was a very good footballer and Jack had been at a tournament watching him play. The next day Jack heard that he had been attacked by a gang on his way home from the tournament. He had been hit on the head with a concrete slab and died.

As Jack told the story he became angry. He walked between the rows of the gang members, shouted at them and challenged them. He knew their gangs and where they were from. He probably knew their dads too. He fired questions at some of them. Which gangs were they in? Were they proud of what they did? Did they think they were hard? Did they think they were brave?

Then he asked some really searching questions: who among them was hard enough to give up the gang fighting? Hard enough to do something better with his life? Hard enough to ring the number? He pointed at an individual and asked him these questions directly. But the man he had singled out just put his head down and avoided Jack's stare. Jack moved on and asked another if he was hard enough. He challenged many of them personally to stand up if they had the bottle to change.

The tension in the court was rising and the atmosphere incredible. Then one young man stood up, then another, then another and Jack kept going. Who else has the courage, who else has the bottle? Within a few minutes every one of the gang members were on their feet making clear their intention to call the number, to try and change. Jack was moving among them encouraging, challenging, praising. The air was electric. I have never experienced such an emotionally charged event in my life and it still wasn't over. As each of the gang members stood up the invited guests began to applaud, quietly at first, as if not to scare anyone. But the applause became even louder and sustained and the gang members on their feet started to applaud too.

This was the dramatic and emotionally charged outcome that I had been sceptical of. I was so wrong.

It was a community coming together. It was different groups hearing the same message at the same time and coming to the same conclusion: we can change this. The violence can stop and we can be better.

The event was over. The gang members left the court clutching the cards with the telephone number. Would they call? Would their inspiration last long enough? We simply didn't know.

Over the next two years we held another ten of these Self

Referral sessions. Jack Black didn't attend any of them. We scripted and refined the message.

The free phone number was used, a lot. The case manage - ment team were very busy. The police formed a gang's task force and that wasn't so busy.

We received a call from a mum whose son was serving a sentence in Polmont Young Offenders Institution. Her son was being released and she wanted to know if he could get involved in the 'gang thing'. We brought some of the young men serving sentences at Polmont to the next couple of sessions and they sat in the dock of the court.

We ran CIRV for two years before handing over responsibility to Strathclyde Police. During that period over six hundred young men and women involved themselves in the initiative. The University of St Andrews evaluated the results for us and they were spectacular.

Among the group involved with CIRV:

Violent offending reduced by	46%
Weapon carrying reduced by	85%
Knife carrying reduced by	58%
Gang fighting reduced by	73%

Some of our partners involved in CIRV also reported great results. For example, in housing the numbers of tenants who were satisfied with their local neighbourhood as a place to live (the CIRV area) increased from 63 per cent to 84 per cent. The percentage of residents NOT feeling safe at night (CIRV area) reduced from 32 per cent to 10 per cent. In education, school exclusions reduced by a staggering 85 per cent. Our health partners also saw significant improvements. For example, the number of hospital admissions for serious violence decreased by 17 per cent and admissions for knife related injuries decreased by 34 per cent.

Near the end of 2009 I received a call from the Police Inspector in Easterhouse who told me that the gang initiative was really working. I said I knew that violence appeared to have reduced substantially and that gang fights were becoming rarer. He agreed. But he also said he was sure the initiative was working because he had received a complaint from a resident of Easterhouse about dog fouling. Now that was a performance indicator even the most ardent MBA junkie wouldn't have thought of.

CIRV received lots of attention not just in Scotland but throughout the UK. After the riots in England in 2011 the Prime Minister, in a speech in the House of Commons, said that they should look to Glasgow to learn how to deal with gangs. The Home Secretary Theresa May and Director of the Home Office Dame Helen Gosh subsequently visited the VRU to hear about our work. Following this visit Karyn and I were invited to become part of the Westminster Government's Anti Gang Task force and we presented on the work of the VRU, including CIRV, to the Inter-Ministerial Group.

There was little doubt that we had made substantial progress and were not only getting results but also inter - national recognition. However, we could not be complacent. We were realising that violence is indeed a 'wicked' problem. Getting the young men to stop fighting was one thing but, as we shall see in the final chapter, making sure they could find a job was almost as big a challenge.

CHAPTER 6
Tackling cultural issues

We realised very early in this journey that the route to a less violent Scotland was neither clear nor straight. At an early meeting about our progress Willie Rae asked us if we had a plan or a map of where we were going. We didn't. I told him that we didn't have a map but we had a compass. We didn't know exactly what we needed to do but we knew for certain that we had to respond differently and that our destination was less violence and fewer victims.

CIRV was just one of the ways we responded differently. We had to be innovative in other areas as well.

Developing an international profile

We knew that one of the biggest priorities for us was to change not only our colleagues' attitudes but also those of other professionals working across the public sector. We also needed to influence politicians and the general public. The media, and our public profile, were key.

We had become members of the World Health Organisation's Violence Prevention Alliance (VPA). Indeed we were the only police members. The VPA is a network of countries, international agencies and community organisations working to reduce violence. Members of the VPA all use an evidence-based public health approach to violence which focuses efforts on risk factors for violence and promotes collaboration and co-operation between agencies. The VPA holds 'milestones' meetings every two years and in 2007 the VRU and the Scottish Government hosted the gathering at the Scottish Police College in Tulliallan.

We had been working very hard to change attitudes about violence – to make everyone think about violence in a different way so hosting a World Health Conference on violence at one of our Police Colleges seemed a powerful symbol of this new thinking. It was a clear statement that in Scotland we not only believed that violence prevention was not the sole responsibility of the police but also that we were serious in our commitment to do something positive about it.

The conference ran for three days in July and the programme was full of authoritative academics and practitioners from around the world. We had an opening reception at Edinburgh Castle addressed by Health Minister Nicola Sturgeon. The Justice Minister, Kenny MacAskill, opened the event at Tulliallan. These two speakers testified that Scotland understood that violence was an issue requiring collaborative responses from heath and justice agencies. It was a powerful message that placed Scotland at the forefront of violence prevention on the world stage.

Other speakers included Vincent Felitti from the USA whose longitudinal studies on Adverse Childhood Experiences, encountered in chapter two, were having a huge impact on primary prevention strategies around the world. Professor Irvin Waller from Canada author of *Less Law More Order* (2006) on evidence-based smart policing strategies also took the podium as did Mary Gordon who had set up Roots of Empathy in Canada.

Jonathon Shepherd who developed the injury surveillance model we were trying to introduce in Scotland also contributed. This model involved the sharing of anonymized health data on violence with police agencies and had been very effective in Cardiff.

George Hosking, the CEO of the WAVE Trust, and Dr Suzanne Zeedyke, a developmental psychologist working, at that time, at Dundee University, also spoke at the event.

And we also heard from important Scottish professionals: Dr Harry Burns, Scotland's Chief Medical Officer, spoke about Scotland's commitment to respond in a different way to violence and the key role that health has to play in violence reduction and prevention and Paddy Tomkins, HM Chief Inspector of Policing in Scotland, confirmed the aspirations of the Scottish police service to really tackle our violence problem. The conference received lots of media coverage and provided the opportunity to talk about violence prevention in a different way. The reporting was well informed and thoughtful.

The conference was a huge success and no doubt helped us really change attitudes but we still had much to do in practical terms to reduce violence.

Prevention is everyone's job

In 2006 we discovered that dental hospitals in Glasgow dealt with a new serious facial injury every six hours. Maxillofacial surgeons and dental surgeons ran the hospital's outpatient clinics. The majority of the injuries they saw were caused by violence and many were repeat victims. Karyn contacted the Glasgow Dental hospital and met with Dr Christine Goodall to discuss what, if anything, we might be able to do about the high number of cases they were dealing with.

We believed that if a patient turned up at a doctor's surgery two or three times a year with a cold, or flu the GP would encourage them to take better care of their health. In other words, they would stress the importance of prevention. But despite the fact that some young men turned up at a facial or dental clinic more than once with different violence related injuries there was no policy or process in place to provide them with advice about prevention. This didn't seem right to us. Karyn had already looked into 'brief motivational interventions'. These are delivered at particular times when patients are motivated to change their behaviour. For example, when a young man is having stitches removed or the wire taken out of his broken jaw he may, at that particular moment, be motivated to think about how his own behaviour might have contributed to his assault. These occasions are often called a 'teachable moment'. The evidence is encouraging as it suggests that advice delivered at such times by a health professional can change the patient's behaviour for the better.

Alcohol plays a significant part in many of the incidents that result in young men being assaulted. We know that alcohol can make people aggressive but often victims are under the influence of alcohol and so don't make good decisions about their safety. For example. they don't walk away when there is a threat or they don't even recognise the threat in the first place. This held true for many of the victims who presented at Glasgow hospitals.

Karyn and Dr Goodall introduced a brief motivational intervention in Glasgow Dental Hospital's clinics. It was delivered by nurses. The first intervention involved identifying those victims who had been drinking at the time of the assault and then trying to make clear to the patient the connection between their drinking and their assault injury. In 2006 there were 1000 facial trauma patients coming into clinics in the west of Scotland and in 2013 that number had halved.

This particular intervention sounds simple yet it is the clearest example of how our thinking about violence was changing. It represented a shift in emphasis from individual responsibility and blame to identification of risk and prevention. The criminal justice model focuses on offenders and sees punishment as a deterrent and a mechanism for behaviour change. On the contrary, the health model acknowledges the causes and risk factors and addresses those to prevent violence.

Dr Goodall, together with colleagues, went on to establish a charity called Medics Against Violence (MAV). The charity is made up of doctors who, like Dr Goodall, were tired of just treating the victims of violence and wanted to do something to prevent them from becoming victims in the first place. These doctors now visit schools and speak to children about violence and its consequences for the victim and the perpetrator. They are highly respected and effective advocates for violence prevention. MAV is supported by the Scottish Government and the VRU and all the doctors and medical professionals give their time for free.

Five years on MAV is still going and still in schools. But it is also now providing domestic abuse training to dentists, vets and the fire service as well as providing training on dealing with rape and sexual assault to GPs and St Andrews First Aid personnel. In short it has widened its focus and is no longer just about young boys running about with knives; it wants to change the culture in relation to violence. In terms of domestic abuse its aim is to encourage as many different groups to provide support and reassurance and to do this in different places. It wants everyone to be talking about the problem – men, women, everyone.

Domestic violence

Domestic violence, particularly violence against women, is a crime which transcends class and culture. If violence in general is to be reduced it is an issue that must be addressed. Even defining what is meant by domestic violence is difficult. It is not solely physical violence but the controlling coercive behaviour of the abuser who will continually undermine and belittle the victim to the extent that the victim not only feels powerless but can be made to feel too that they deserve what is happening to them. This is why it's often very difficult for a victim to leave her abuser. Often there are children in the relationship making leaving even more difficult.

It is common in households with domestic violence for children to witness the abuse. Most young men serving a sentence in Polmont Young Offenders Institution will have witnessed domestic abuse in their childhood. This does not necessarily mean that they will themselves become abusers but it does mean that they are more likely to become abusers themselves.

For agencies one of the most challenging aspects of domestic violence is that it usually takes place in private and victims very seldom report incidents to the police. There has never been a national prevalence study in Scotland so we don't know for certain how common abuse actually is. Estimates suggest that as many one in five women will be the victim of domestic abuse at some time in her life. A woman may suffer up to 34 incidents of violence before she finds the courage to leave and ask for help. From experience I believe that these estimates vastly underestimate the levels of domestic violence in our culture. I also think it is critically important that we continue to push for a national prevalence study, as we need an accurate diagnosis if we are to respond adequately and effectively.

The VRU's response to domestic violence was to tackle it in a number of different ways. In 2008 we jointly sponsored a visit to Scotland by Professor Jackson Katz. Katz is an American academic who advocates 'the bystander approach' to gender violence and bullying prevention. He has developed a programme called 'Mentors in Violence Prevention' (MVP). What is different about Katz's approach is that rather than focusing on women as victims and men as perpetrators of harassment, abuse or violence, he concentrates on the role of peers in schools, groups, teams and workplaces. In short, he focuses on bystanders.

Katz is a powerful speaker and spoke at several conferences and events during his visit. He contends, convincingly, that since the overwhelming majority of perpetrators of violence against women are men then violence against women is an issue for *men* to deal with and resolve. It is not enough for men to claim they don't assault women rather they must speak up, and condemn, those who do. Moreover they must challenge sexist language, inappropriate and sexist jokes and gender inequality. It is by doing this that they will change the culture – a culture which not only permits violence against women but supports and validates it in many people's minds. This is very different from the usual approach to domestic violence which sees it primarily as a 'women's issue'.

Working with the national body Education Scotland the VRU established MVP in several schools. The programme aims to develop positive relationships and create an inclusive culture in schools which proactively prevents and deals with all types of bullying behaviour. For example, MVP uses a creative bystander approach to challenge bullying behaviour such as 'sexting', dating violence and sexual harassment. The MVP programme does not identify individuals as perpetrators or victims but as empowered bystanders who can support their friends and classmates. It also trains High School mentors to deliver peer to peer sessions to younger pupils in the school.

There was another, very different, approach which we also promoted. Remember that our aim is to prevent violence from happening and this does not always require inter - vention by the police. Victims of domestic abuse are usually too afraid to report it for fear of being further victimised or assaulted by their partners. So the problem is how can we reach them? Other professionals, particularly dentists, are often better placed to pick up the telltale signs and provide support. Research has shown that when female dental patients have a bruise on their face they are 32 times more likely to have this injury as a result of domestic violence than any other cause. Women visiting the dentist are also more likely to feel safe talking to the dentist about the abuse than other professionals such as police officers or social workers because they know their confidences are not going to be betrayed.

This was why we worked with Medics Against Violence to train over 600 dentists to identify the signs of domestic abuse and signpost victims to help and support. The method we trained them to use is called AVDR:

A   **ask**

V   **validate**

D   **document**

R   **refer**

This method is founded on one used in the United States. It involves the dentist asking the patient about any suspicious injuries which they see during the examination. They do this without making any judgement. If an incident is disclosed the dentist documents the injuries and, if the patient agrees, the dentist may photograph the injuries. Incidents are only reported to the police if the victim wants this to happen. What is most important is that the victim can talk to someone and get help and support. It's about reducing the number of victims. It's about prevention and not about reported crime statistics.

Strategic plan

As part of our efforts to change attitudes and encourage collaborative action we wrote and published a ten year strategic plan. It was launched by Justice Minister Kenny MacAskill and Stephen House, the new Chief Constable of

Strathclyde in 2008. The plan set out to reflect our commitment to treat violence as a public health issue.

As I have explained throughout the VRU had only very limited direct control over the police in Strathlcyde and we had no control over the development and delivery of local resources in 32 local authorities, 7 police forces or 14 health boards. All we could do was try to influence outwith our authority. The ten year plan was our attempt to do that.

The plan included our aims in six distinct areas:

1 Violence reduction as a national priority

2 Enforcement

3 Attitudinal change

4 Primary prevention – seeking to prevent the onset of violence or to change behaviour so that violence is prevented from developing

5 Secondary prevention – to halt the progression of violence once it is established. This would be achieved by early detection or early diagnosis followed by prompt effective treatment

6 Tertiary prevention – the rehabilitation of people with an established violent behaviour or who have been affected as a victim.

We wanted the plan to serve as a framework for securing support and approval for detailed planning. We hoped that by outlining our aspirations for violence prevention we would motivate others.

We sent copies of our plan to every director in every local authority, every Director of Public Health in every health board, every Chief Constable in every police force and every

MSP and MP in Scotland. We asked that the plan be used to inform local planning, and that violence prevention was prioritised.

Several local authorities and several directors contacted us to say that they had found the plan useful and that they had used it to help with their local planning. This was the best we could hope for, but given the scale of the challenge, far short of what was required to make a sizeable difference.

Two examples illustrate how much still needed to be done.

People in Cardiff have developed a model of injury surveillance with good evaluations and the ability to reduce violence. Information is anonymised and shared with police. In 2007 we began an injury surveillance pilot in three A & E departments in Lanarkshire, based on the Cardiff model. The VRU employed an analyst and paid for IT fixes. We held meet - ings, conferences, enrolled the support of the Chief Medical Officer. We demonstrated its effectiveness yet it is still not fully in place Scotland wide and operating eight years on.

We had great support from individuals within the hospitals and in the health board, but as it is not a designated health target it is not therefore a health priority.

Secondly the VRU had taken on the national role for violence reduction in 2006. This involved coordinating a national campaign of operational policing activity and to do this we formed the national Tactical Violence Reduction Group (TVRG). This group had representatives from all the police forces in Scotland including the British Transport Police and the Ministry of Defence Police.

We were funded by the Scottish Government and

Strathclyde Police and recognised by the Association of Chief Police Officers Scotland (ACPOS) but we had no direct mandate or authority to order individual Chief Constables to do anything or even to prioritise operational activity. All we could do was coordinate and the TVRG was the mechanism to do this nationally. Through the TVRG we agreed specific themes related to violence – weapons, alcohol and public space violence and domestic abuse. The campaigns were run under the Safer Scotland banner.

Representation on the TVRG varied between forces, some appointing Superintendents others appointing Sergeants. This variance in seniority of representatives demonstrated the variance in support and commitment from the different forces for our work. I should say though that, thankfully, the enthusiasm and commitment of the representatives did not necessarily relate in any way to their rank.

However, it is also true to say that many were reluctant members of the TVRG even though every Chief Constable in Scotland, through ACPOS, supported it. At times this was hugely frustrating.

There were some who believed that violence was only a problem for Strathclyde. It was a 'Weedgie' thing (Glaswegian), and therefore anything we had to say on the matter would be irrelevant to their particular local context.

On reflection, I recall that some police offers from other forces in Scotland used to consider Strathclyde Police as the enemy. For them its size was a threat; the experience of its officers irrelevant; and its influence unhealthy and counter to the common good. These individuals considered there was nothing that Strathclyde was doing that would apply to their area. They were different but just as smart and just as clever as any Weedgie. This type of resistance made our task of winning people over more difficult.

CHAPTER 7

A wicked problem

Every issue no matter how narrow and every subject no matter how small will have been researched, studied, defined, catalogued and written about by academics somewhere. Violence is no exception. There are mountains of papers, publications and books about why people are violent, how people are violent and different definitions of every type of violence – intimate partner violence, interpersonal violence, self directed violence, collective violence. These experts even define the circumstances that will increase the risk of violence as the determinants and causes are also well researched and defined.

However, while academics can comprehensively define the problem, effective solutions are far less readily available and examples of such solutions being successfully applied are even more difficult to find. I suspect this is one reason why simple, punitive and blunt criminal justice responses have established such a dominant position in relation to how we respond to violence. This also seems true in relation to crime and criminality more generally. Criminal justice solutions should be the service response of last resort. Instead they have become the service response of first resort. This has led to the common belief that more police, more prisons, more legislation will fix the problem, any problem. Yet where is the supporting evidence?

I think most professionals working in criminal justice realise its serious shortcomings and ineffectiveness. I am certain that the public too understand that prevention is better than cure. Nonetheless we persist with punitive responses and the criminalization of behaviour and people.

Shifting our practice

During an election in Scotland I was asked by David Leask, a reporter with *The Herald*, if I thought that the promise of an extra 1000 police officers being made by one of the contending parties would be a good idea. I said that it would be a great idea. Of course it would. We can always use more people. But I then qualified my response by saying that while 1000 extra cops would be a great idea, 1000 extra health visitors would be a clever idea. I expected to be challenged on this. David Leask thought so too but I wasn't. And this was a key moment for me and not just because my comments made me very popular with health visitors.

I now realise that even when we know what the right thing is, we don't always do it. It's as if we are stuck in a permafrost of caution. We are striving not so much to keep everyone happy but not to upset anyone.

Violence, unlike many other crimes, is about human behaviour so prevention or reduction requires us to think about how we might change how people behave and that's not easy.

When we think about this we usually start by asking how humans learn to be violent. This is a reasonable question and good place to start but I think it makes much more sense to turn that question on its head and ask how it is humans learn *not* to be violent.

If we are born into a stable, loving environ ment that provides a positive early years experience, we learn and develop other human attributes: the non-cognitive skills I spoke of earlier. We learn to communicate, to negotiate, to compromise, to problem solve. We learn how to empathise and so the violence option becomes the last choice on our tactical options menu. We retain the violence option but it exists alongside a whole suite of other responses available to us. Effectively this makes the need to resort to violence almost redundant. In other words, we learn to navigate life, establish and maintain good relationships and make good decisions about ourselves, so that the violence option is not required.

So many of the violent young men I have encountered were not making the conscious decision to choose violence. For them violence was their only choice. It's the only response they know. Not only is violence their *only* choice, that choice has been reinforced as an appropriate choice by their daily experience. This then takes us back to the importance of people's early years experience to everything that happens to them throughout life.

Thinking about viiolence in this way allows a clearer under-standing of how we might prevent it. It offers the opportunity to develop and apply different responses. Essentially this is what we did and it's what the Violence Reduction Unit continues to do: think about things in a different way, and try to do the right things that can make a difference.

Developing different responses is only one part of the challenge. Implementing these new responses is even more crucial and this proved far more difficult than we had thought. As I have already said, I thought people would do the right thing simply because it was the right thing to do. But I was wrong.

There's no doubt that violence is a complex and complicated problem. This leads some to believe that our responses require to be equally complex and complicated. However, I came to see that some people make the solutions to violence complex and complicated, not because they have to be, but in order to demonstrate how clever they are. Personally I think our responses should only be as complicated as they need to be to succeed and nothing more.

Defining wicked problems

Willie Rae often spoke to us about violence being 'a wicked problem'. At first I thought his use of the word wicked meant that violence was evil. But he explained that the term 'wicked problems' related to a type of particular public policy problems.

In the 1970s social planners coined the term 'wicked problems' to refer to complex problems which unlike 'tame problems' (such as how to win a chess game or find the answer to a mathematical puzzle) are very difficult to solve. Many contemporary social problems such as drug-taking, domestic violence, or worklessness are wicked in that they are highly connected, cannot be completely eliminated, and any solution is never right or wrong, simply better or worse. As there are no solutions as such, what might work somewhere at a specific point in time may not be transferable to another area or context.

The principal researchers in this area are two Urban Planners formerly from the University of Berkeley, Horst Rittel and Melvin Webber. If I briefly list the key characteristics they ascribe to wicked problems it's easy to see how violence can be defined as a wicked problem:

1 There is no clear definition of a wicked problem.

2 Our actions can make wicked problems better or worse.

3 It's not clear when a wicked problem is fixed.

4 Every attempt to fix a wicked problem will change it.

Remember that there's no clear definition of violence – it can take many forms from bullying to suicide. Criminal justice people are concerned with violent crimes but aren't interested in suicide or even certain types of bullying. Also as we've seen there's massive under-reporting of violence which makes under standing the scale very difficult and reported crime figures are not a dependable or accurate measure. Even knowing if we are making the problem better or worse is at best guesswork.

When we respond only with criminal justice solutions we can often make things worse. This is particularly true in relation to domestic violence as arresting an abuser and punishing him does not necessarily stop the abuse when he is released. In fact it may become worse.

When we respond we can often change the problem or partially fix it but in fixing one problem we can often create another. For example, police stop and search tactics can be effective in stopping violence through confiscating weapons or prosecuting young men for carrying them. But when that tactic becomes the principal response it can create other issues.

This is particularly true when tactics such as stop and search are used within a culture of performance manage - ment where numbers become the measure of success. The police target a particular group which is then repeatedly stopped and searched. This action then risks alienating them from the police and their community. In Scotland the targeted group has been young white men living in deprived areas. Stop and search is a legitimate and effective policing tactic but it must be smart, focused and proportionate. More importantly we must not be afraid to change tactics when circumstances change, and police in a different way.

The employment problem

The success of the CIRV gang project in Glasgow also created new problems. The young men who decided to stop gang fighting and carrying weapons needed jobs, but a previous conviction is often a barrier to gaining employment. It is important to realise that not all violent men are caught and have a criminal record. Some of the men involved in gang violence were still able to hold down a job. Remember not all violence is reported and the police mostly catch the feckless and the stupid.

However, as the police became more interested in gang fighting, alcohol abuse and anti social behaviour more young men were likely to get caught and convicted of a breach of the peace or vandalism or even a minor assault. Such convictions then prevent them from getting jobs. However, the direct relevance of the conviction to the job can often be difficult to fathom. I can understand a convicted fraudster not being given a job with responsibility for money or a paedophile not being given a job looking after children. But I don't understand a young man with a conviction for breach of the peace being prevented from working as labourer on a building site, for example.

In 2009 the UK Government made funding available to provide for short-term jobs. In Scotland there was funding for about fifty jobs and these jobs were only for six months. The intention was to allow young people, who would have otherwise found it difficult to get a job, to gain work experience. Hopefully the employer may even keep them on full time at the end of the six months.

One young man from the Barlanark area of Glasgow got one of these jobs working as a refuse collector in Glasgow. He had been on the CIRV project and we helped him get a job on this scheme. Every day for six months he cycled from Barlanark to the depot which was about four miles each way. He was twenty-one years old, it was his first job and he never missed a day. He was such a good worker that his local supervisor told him to fill in an application form for a full time position. He also told him that he would give him his full support and he was almost sure that he would get the job. When he was offered the job full time, he was ecstatic.

Just a few months earlier such an outcome would have been beyond his wildest dreams.

As part of the standard application process the young man had to complete a disclosure check form. Before he could start, his disclosure report came back showing that he had three previous convictions, the most recent was three years old and all were for minor offences. The job offer was withdrawn immediately. He turned up at the VRU offices the morning he learned the news, distraught. The CIRV team worked hard to support him. Fortunately he now has another job, not collecting refuse.

The Human Resources Department at the council followed all the HR processes as well as HR legislation. They were followed to the letter but the outcome completely alienated a young man denied employment because he was caught committing minor crimes when he was a teenager. The job he was applying for and for which he had clearly demonstrated his ability was emptying dustbins.

Our experience in trying to engage and work with the thirty-two local authorities, fourteen health boards, eight police forces and countless third sector organisations confirmed the validity of Sir Willie's description of violence as a wicked problem.

Of course, there are countless numbers of individuals in many organisations, public, private and third sector, who work heroically every day to make a difference and make things better for the folk they serve. But sadly they are often working within constrictive and controlling structures that inhibit positive outcomes. What's more, the processes and working practices appear to have been designed to benefit the organisation and not the recipient of the services.

These different organisations, and the policies and processes they create, can be as corrosive, damaging and limiting as the youth gangs that used to blight the east end of Glasgow. They are territorial. They have their own language. They are bound by rigid rules that are often used by them as a defence against change. Some too possess a collective arrogance that rejects the notion that anyone outside their 'gang' could even understand what their challenges are. The idea that an outsider might know a better way of doing things is absurd and insulting. My experience leads me to believe that they often keep things complicated and complex as a defence against anyone just doing the simple things that would make things better.

Career moves

I retired from the police in February 2013, just before the creation of Police Scotland. While it felt strange not being a police officer after almost forty years, I knew there was still much to do to change attitudes and convince others of the shared agenda so I left the VRU with the intention of continuing the journey. I worked at the University of St Andrews supporting the VRU, trying to ensure our collective understanding of what we had learned about reducing violence was used to inform and improve collaborative practice across Scotland.

I left St Andrews in 2014 and set up a website called Responding Differently which I hope will help change attitudes and encourage some disruptive innovation.

(www.respondingdifferently.com) I'm also still asked to speak about our journey at conferences and events through - out Scotland and abroad and I do that.

I remain committed to continuing to do what I can to help reduce violence. I find now that my experience allows me the opportunity to challenge the negative attitudes and complex and complicated practices that have been used consistently but with limited success for so long.

CHAPTER 8

My convictions

Karyn and I set up the Violence Reduction Unit in 2004.
We did so as we were encouraged, supported and inspired
by the vision of Willie Rae who was confident enough, smart
enough and brave enough to confront Glasgow's violence
problem and do the right thing.

Here are the Scottish figures from a decade ago and the
latest figures:

Table1: Comparison of murders and assaults in Scotland 2004/5 and 2013/14

	2004/05	2013/14
Murders	142	61
Attempt murders	828	317
Serious assaults	6,775	2,951
Simple assaults	73,711	60,357

These are testimony to the fact that the various actions and
programmes described in this book have, literally, saved lives.

Violence figures have, however, fallen in most of the western
world so some may question whether the Scottish figures

merely reflect this trend. Crime figures are notoriously difficult to compare because it can be hard to establish baseline figures. For example, the various categories of assault are defined in different ways in different countries and the definitions change. Homicide is a more reliable figure for comparison. If we use the Home Office Homicide Index to compare figures between Scotland and England and Wales then we can see quite clearly that Scotland's homicide rate is improving at a faster rate than it is south of the border.

Table 2: Reduction of homicide rates in England and Wales and Scotland from 2004/5 to 2013/14

| England & Wales | 32 per cent reduction |
| Scotland | 57 per cent reduction |

Despite this improvement in Scotland's murder rate I am aware of the continuing challenges facing young men, and their families, in the areas which have traditionally been blighted by violence. Many of the poorest and most deprived areas in the UK are in Scotland, particularly Glasgow. Most of these areas have been struggling for decades and remain deprived despite the investment of millions upon millions of pounds in redevelopment over many years.

We have one of the most comprehensive and free social support systems in the world. We have a universal and free health service. We have free education. Yet, despite all of these services and support systems, many still fail to live healthy and fruitful lives. Violence may be down but it hasn't disappeared as an issue and there are still significant problems when it comes to health, employment and education. Ambition is woefully low in many of our deprived communities.

Indeed given the programmes, services and investment we must conclude that the problems are not simply about money or resources.

So what might make a difference? Throughout the book I've continually mentioned the early years. Scotland now has a key Scottish Government project called the 'Early Years Collaborative'. This is part of a national commitment to 'make Scotland the best place to grow up'. Given my conviction that people's early years experience has a huge impact on their future lives I welcome this development. However, I think that in Scotland we still have some way to go to change attitudes. Sometimes I think we don't actually like children and that perhaps we only tolerate them.

I also think there is a tension in the Scottish Government's approach to young children. On the one hand they say they want to put the good of children first while in their childcare strategy they are more motivated by getting women back to work after childbirth, and growing the economy, than in providing an enriching early years experience for all children. Personally I believe that if we are serious about early years we should be providing at least two years' paid paternity leave that can be shared between mum and dad.

I also welcome the Scottish Government's health plans to increase the number of Health Visitors by five hundred. It is a good start though this initiative will only make a difference if Health Visitors are permitted and supported to do what they are good at – helping families and parents be as good as they can be.

I also support the Scottish Government's plans to introduce minimum unit pricing for alcohol. This won't change things overnight but nonetheless it could make a difference. Importantly it shows that our politicians recognise the negative impact alcohol can have and their willingness to do something about it despite lobbying, complaints and legal action from the drinks industry.

There are lots of other policy and fiscal changes that could be made that could help Scotland tackle inequality and become fairer. However, I believe that there are some subtle changes which may help us become more effective.

Asking an important question

At the VRU we always used to ask two questions when confronting any particular problem. 'What do we want to achieve?' and 'How are we going to achieve it?'

It's important that we define the desired outcome – the What – at the outset as this lets us work back from that point. By doing this we can identify which partners will be required and what the role of each partner will be in delivering the single agreed outcome, the How. This process helps us to establish which organisation or agency is best equipped, or best placed, to deliver that outcome.

Working in partnership has taught me to ask a third and vitally important question and that's *Why* is it we want to do it. The Why question is important because it will define the level and focus of commitment.

The Why question is hugely important if collaborations are required as partners must all agree at the outset, Why they are committing to a particular project, initiative or change.

Asking the Why question reveals faulty thinking. Indeed, as well as the Scottish Government's childcare strategy, I can think of a few national strategies where the Why question exposes flaws. For example, the ethos of community sentencing is sound and its effectiveness in reducing reoffending is well evidenced. So we should do it. But often the reason we are doing it is to save on the cost of prisons. The result is short term cash savings rather than a reduction in recidivism. If we concentrated more on the latter I'm sure our results would be much better.

If we are serious we should invest in community sentencing because it will reduce reoffending, crime, and prison numbers and help more people get into jobs so that they can lead independent lives and contribute to society and the economy.

Putting professionalism in perspective

Over the years I've repeatedly seen the emphasis senior managers in organisations place on technical and professional skills. I find it worrying that so many professionals believe they just need to do more of the same and everything will be ok; that what we need is more policy, more training and more processes and problems will be fixed. This slavish adherence to professional process is naïvely arrogant and hopelessly ineffective. Not only does it ignore the value of human attributes but it often deliberately devalues them by seeing them as 'unprofessional'.

I don't think that good frontline care workers, in any role, can do their jobs unless they take their whole self to work every day. To do their job properly they need to employ their compassion, their empathy, and their humanity. They need to care. Of course, they also need the time to care, the time to establish relationships, and the time to make a difference. We have to realise that being a frontline care worker is not just a job. It requires humanity, empathy and strength of character to make the difficult decisions, to have the hard conversations and to confront the uncomfortable truths.

I'm not saying that technical skills are not important but I am saying that they are not more important than the human attributes that demand we care for our fellow humans. By allying the technical skills with the human attributes we will produce far more robust and caring services. I've never read a conclusion to a serious case review that said we didn't know what to do. We always seem to know what to do; it's just that sometimes we don't actually do it.

The role of policy and process is to support workers so that they can do their job, whether that is as a social worker, nurse, health visitor, teacher or police officer. Aristotle said that 'moral wisdom' is made up of moral skill, knowing what to do, and moral will, actually doing it. I agree.

All this leads me to believe that we need less professional development not more. We need fewer policies and less upskilling of the workforce. Our policies and supporting processes must allow employees to act more easily as compassionate, caring individuals who use their humanity to work out the best course of action.

Connection

The human brain has huge capacity. Most of that capacity is designed to establish and maintain relationships with other humans. Our brains are literally designed to help us connect with other human beings. This is why we are so adept at reading other people's body language and recognising emotions in facial expressions. We need each other to survive and thrive. Loneliness is as big a killer as tobacco smoke. Without connection we are alienated and lost. Gang members connect with each other because no one else connects with them as individuals. People who are not cared for, don't care.

Every day now I see evidence of this human drive for connection. The Commonweath Games 2014 is a fine example. I sat on my settee, watching the athletes exert themselves beyond breaking. Watching their reactions when they won or lost, I found myself sharing their emotions, their tears of joy, their tears of disappointment. I was watching TV in my own home, crying with Lynsey Sharp and Jo Pavey. I don't even know them, I wasn't even there and Jo is English. I couldn't help myself. I was connected. I'm human.

Connection is how my brain works. I was connected to these athletes – just like I was connected to the families of murder victims and to the families of the murderers I arrested. Connection is not a conscious choice. It takes no effort. It's just the way we are, or at least how we are meant to be. To stay confidently connected, though, we need the help of other people.

There is a young man called James who works with Karyn and her team at the VRU. James has had a very difficult life and is now a fine example of what humans are capable of. I heard him speak to an audience that included the First Minister of Scotland. He said, 'I'm only here today because people like you care for people like me'. Immediately, the atmosphere in the room shifted. As a result the whole audience felt connected to James and to each other.

Reflecting on the past ten years and the changes that have happened in Scotland around violence prevention I am convinced that these reductions in violence represent the efforts and energies of a whole range of agencies and groups. But I think at its heart the changes have been made by people connected to other people who challenge the status quo and people who want to make things better.

Any success that the VRU has had was only possible because people connected around a single cause, a shared agenda and that was reducing violence to make Scotland safer. Like us those involved believed that violence is truly a wicked problem but that it's not inevitable – it's preventable.

A famous slogan from Bill Clinton's 1992 presidential election campaign tells us 'It's the economy, stupid.' Well all my experience at the VRU has led me to a very different conclusion. It's not the economy which we should be trying to fix. It's relationships.

Afterword by Karyn McCluskey

It's quite an experience reading a book that encapsulates over ten years of your life. It describes the most difficult, stressful challenges we undertook and without doubt some of the most life affirming.

At the very outset I want to mention the families of victims who came through our doors, for they are the reason John and I started this – John Muir, Bea Jones, Joyce Young, Maureen Douglas to mention but a very few, for there are hundreds of families out there, all grieving, regardless of the time elapsed. I wish that our paths had never crossed, that they had never had to meet John or me. Alongside these families are those people who suffer life changing injury through violence and abuse. Detection of a crime is essential, but preventing it in the first place is critical.

If the violence reduction agenda is about anything, it was and is, about making things happen. T. S. Eliot, in *The Hollow Men*, conveys the shadow of paralysis that can prevent us taking action. It is in the shadows that things fail. Where we fail to achieve our goals because we are too fearful of the journey, too risk averse, unsure of our skills, and the most cataclysmic of all the 'terror of error'.

When Obama was running for presidency in 2007 he talked about the 'smallness of our politics' and what he said stayed with me in relation to our journey in violence reduction.

> What's stopped us from meeting challenges is not
> the absence of sound policies and sensible plans.
> What's stopped us is the failure of leadership, the
> smallness of our politics – the ease with which
> we're distracted by the petty and trivial, our chronic
> avoidance of tough decisions, our preference for
> scoring cheap political points instead of rolling up
> our sleeves and building a working consensus to
> tackle big problems.

Whilst Obama was considering the big politics in the U.S., the same was true in Scotland: we tried to engage everyone and anyone, the naysayers and the heroes, in equal measure. John and I decided we couldn't let our fear and risk averseness keep us from thinking about different ways to achieve a better outcome in relation to both victims and offenders, and for Scotland.

On a personal note I believe that all of us in violence reduction just wanted to 'lean in' to the challenge of an intractable problem and try to do our best. We met so many outstanding people involved in all walks of life who have been part of the change (you know who you are). John and I tried our very best, and I am so grateful for the last decade. It's been exhausting!

I know Scotland is better now, I know Scotland is safer now, but we are not there yet. Too many lives are still blighted by violence, there can be no complacency. We must keep trying, all of us, for we are presented with the opportunity to make some real change: to change the destiny of some of the most excluded in our country and to improve their lives, and those of their children. This is within our grasp.

This book on violence reduction is about people, particularly engaging the most alienated, and it is their stories that keep us on this path. We recently interviewed a young woman for a work programme. She had been addicted to drugs but was now clean. She had spent many years in prostitution, never had an interview and was covered in self harm marks. We asked that old interview staple 'why should we take you?' To which she replied 'Oh, I wouldn't take me'. So we did. A young man walked five miles to our office on his birthday, arriving at 10am, just to get a chance to be part of something, then walked five miles back home. We took him too.

Many of our offenders have children and we know that a high percentage of children of offenders also end up taking the same path. The one thing we must do is to make it better for the children. They need to see their parents fulfilled, happy, part of something, proud. Starting a job may begin a real change in their lives and that's worth doing.

John Cleese once said 'It's not the despair. I can take the despair. It's the hope I can't stand.' Well, I think we could all do with a little hope.

Karyn McCluskey, 2015

References and links

I have listed below the main documents and websites related to material I cite in the book. I have done this in order of the citation. This list (including live web links) is also on the Conviction page of the Postcards from Scotland website. http://www.postcardsfromscotland.co.uk/book_09.html

The Violence Reduction Unit
http://www.actiononviolence.org.uk
This website will provide links to all of the references, publications, people, evaluations and reports mentioned.

James Garbarino
http://www.apbspeakers.com/speaker/james-garbarino

Homicide in Scotland 2013–14 – Statistical Bulletin Crime & Justice Series 2013–14
http://www.scotland.gov.uk/Resource/0046/00465657.pdf

The World Report on Violence and Health – Geneva: WHO
http://www.who.int/violence_injury_prevention/violence/wor ld_report/en/

Violence Prevention Alliance
http://www.who.int/violenceprevention/en/
This website provides an excellent library of initiatives, interventions and projects from around the world which have been evaluated as effective.

Violence prevention: An invitation to inter-sectorial action
http://www.who.int/violenceprevention/about/
intersectoral_ action.pdf

The Wave Report 2005: Violence and what to do about it
http://www.wavetrust.org

Report of the ministerial task force on health inequalities
Scottish Government 2008
http://www.gov.scot/Publications/2008/06/25104032/0

Information on the Scottish Government's Early Years Collaborative
http://www.gov.scot/Topics/People/Young-People/earlyyears/
early-years-collaborative

Dr Vincent J Felitti
http://acestudy.org

The Adverse Childhood Experiences (ACE) Study
http://www.cdc.gov/violenceprevention/acestudy/
index.html

WHO Milestones event at The Scottish Police College 2007
MacAskill K (2007) Tackling Violence in Scotland
http://www.scotland.gov.uk/News/Speeches/Speeches/
Saferand- stronger/violence
http://www.who.int/violenceprevention/events/17_07_2007/
en/

The Cincinnati Initiative to Reduce Violence
http://www.cincinnati-oh.gov/police/
communityinvolvement/ cincinnati-initiative-to-reduce-
violence/

CIRV Glasgow
Addressing gang-related violence in Glasgow: A preliminary pragmatic quasi-experimental evaluation of the Community Initiative to Reduce Violence (CIRV). Aggression and Violent Behavior 19(6): 686-691.
http://www.sciencedirect.com/science/article/pii/
S1359178914001074

Professor Irvin Waller
http://irvinwaller.org

Professor Richard Tremblay
http://www.prevnet.ca/about/team/board-of-directorsadvisory/ dr-richard-tremblay

Dr Suzanne Zeedyke
http://suzannezeedyk.co.uk/wp2/

Professor James Heckman
http://heckmanequation.org

Medics Against Violence
http://medicsagainstviolence.co.uk

Mentors in Violence Prevention programme (MVP)
http://jacksonkatz.com
http://www.jacksonkatz.com/mvp.html

Wicked Problems
http://www.uctc.net/mwebber/Rittel+Webber+Dilemmas+General_Theory_of_Planning.pdf

Injury Surveillance – The Cardiff Model
http://www.college.police.uk/About/What-do-we-offer/
Documents/RR-851-CoP_AE_Guidance_report_final.pdf

Scottish Government (2009b) *Changing Scotland's relationship with alcohol: A framework for action.* Available at http://www.scotland.gov.uk/Resource/Doc/262905/0078610.pdf

Scottish Government (2009c) *Safer lives: Changed lives. A shared approach to tackling violence against women in Scotland.* Available at http://www.scotland.gov.uk/Resource/Doc/274212/0082013.pdf

1. AfterNow – What next for a healthy Scotland?
| *Phil Hanlon/Sandra Carlisle*
The authors of this visionary book look at health in Scotland and beyond health to the main social, economic, environmental and cultural challenges of our times. They examine the type of transformational change required to create a more resilient and healthy Scotland.

2. The Great Takeover – How materialism, the media and markets now dominate our lives | *Carol Craig*
Describes the dominance of materalist values, the media and business in all our lives and how this is leading to a loss of individual and collective well-being. It looks at many of the big issues of our times – debt, inequality, political apathy, loss of self-esteem, pornography and the rise of celebrity culture. The conclusion is simple and ultimately hopeful – we can change our values and our lives.

3. The New Road – Charting Scotland's inspirational communities | *Alf Young/Ewan Young*
A father and son go on a week long journey round Scotland to see at first hand some of the great environmental, social, employment and regeneration projects which are happening. From Dunbar in the south east of Scotland to Knoydart in the north west they meet people involved in projects which demonstrate new ways of living.

4. Scotland's Local Food Revolution | *Mike Small*
Lifts the lid on the unsavoury reality of our current food system including horsemeat in processed beef products, the unsustainable movement of food round the globe, and how supermarket shopping generates massive waste. It's an indictment of a food syste that is out of control. But there is hope – the growth and strength of Scotland's local food movement.

5. Letting Go – Breathing new life into organisations | *Tony Miller/Gordon Hall*
It is now commonplace for employees to feel frustrated at work – ground down by systems that are dominated by rules, protocols, guidelines, targets and inspections. Tony Miller and Gordon Hall explore the origins of 'command and control' management as well as the tyranny of modern day 'performance management'. Effective leaders, they argue, should 'let go' of their ideas on controlling staff and nurture intrinsic motivation instead.

6. Raising Spirits – Allotments, well-being and community | *Jenny Mollison/Judy Wilkinson/Rona Wilkinson*
Allotments are the unsung story of our times; hidden places for food, friendship and freedom from the conformity of everyday life. A fascinating look at how allotments came about; why they can make such a substantial contribution to health, well-being, community, food production, and the environment; and what's happening in other countries.

7. Schooling Scotland – Education, equity and community | *Daniel Murphy*
The Scottish schooling system does well for many children growing up in Scotland, but to ensure that all children get the education they deserve, a better partnership of parent, child, school, government and society is needed – one to which all Scotland can contribute and from which all children can benefit. Daniel Murphy suggests eight ways to ensure that Scottish education could be stronger and fairer.

8. Shaping our Global Future – A guide for young people | *Derek Brown*
Young people worry about the future world they will live in: personal futures, families and jobs. But they also worry about their global futures. The possibilities and challenges ahead appear overwhelming. This guide to human achievements and future challenges is designed to help young people consider the future their children and grandchildren will inhabit.

9. Conviction – Violence, culture and a shared public service agenda | *John Carnochan*
Policeman John Carnochan takes us on a memorable journey of discovery as he comes to grips with violence and Scotland's traditionally high murder rate. He also gives a fascinating insight into the work of Scotland's Violence Reduction Unit and why it has

been so spectacularly successful. This compelling book is not about high visibility policing or more officers but the importance of empathy and children's early years.

10. She, He, They – Families, gender and coping with transition | Shirley Young

How challenging can gender transition be for both parents and siblings? A story of hope and resilience, it shows that if parents can move beyond the shock and pain of their offspring's transition, all family members can come closer together and experience life-enhancing change.

11. Knowing and Growing – Insights for developing ourselves and others | Alan McLean

This extraordinary book provides insights and practical tools to help you navigate everyday human interactions, balance your own and others' needs and utilise your emotions to create a more fulfilling life. The powerful insights readers glean from 'McLean's Ring' are not only helpful for parents, teachers and leaders they are also essential for anyone aiming to encourage others to grow and develop as individuals.

12. Working for Equality – Policy, politics people | Richard Freeman, Fiona McHardy, Danny Murphy (Editors)

Brings together 22 experienced practitioners from across the country to reflect on equality/inequality – in class, race, gender, poverty, disability and homelessness as well as health and education. They are concerned about individuals as well as ideas and policy instruments. Short and accessible, a pause for thought and inspiration for those concerned with action.

13. Hiding in Plain Sight – Exploring Scotland's ill health | Carol Craig

Scotland. A country that prides itself on its modernity and progressive instincts. Yet this is a nation whose mental and physical health outcomes are poor by European standards. This book asks why? Grippingly readable yet challenging, Carol Craig offers an answer which is glaringly obvious. Generations of Scottish children have suffered in ways that undermine the nation's health. Starting from her own and her neighbours' lives, she explores the growing awareness internationally of the impact of Adverse Childhood Experiences.

14. Right from the Start – Investing in parents and babies | *Alan Sinclair*
Scotland languishes in the second division of global child well-being. One child in every four is judged to be 'vulnerable' when they enter primary school. Alan Sinclair reveals the harm inflicted on so many of our youngest, most defenceless citizens through a toxic mix of poor parenting, bad health and a society focussed on dealing with consequences rather than causes. He also sets out a routemap for us to start putting children first by helping us all to become better parents.

15. The Golden Mean – fostering young people's resilience, confidence and well-being | *Morag Kerr (Editor)*
How do we encourage children and young people and help foster the skills they need to thrive in our increasingly complex world? This insightful and stimulating collection of writings by activists, people who work with the young, commentators and young people themselves provides a compelling answer. We need to strike a healthy balance between support and challenge – 'the golden mean'.

16. The Dear Wild Place | *Emily Cutts*
This book recounts the frenetic campaign to protect a magical oasis in the heart of a busy city from housing development – a David and Goliath struggle. Shows how a grassroots initiative can address the intensive materialism of modern life, improve children's lives, provide precious outdoor space for play and health, build a vibrant community and break down barriers caused by pronounced income inequality. An inspiration to all.

17. Play is the Way – Child development, early years and the future of Scottish education | *Sue Palmer (ed)*
Always the Cinderella of the education system, the significance of early years has been seriously under-estimated. **Play is the Way** brings together leading practitioners, policy-makers and academics to explain how a coherent approach to early years – centred on positive relationships and play – will not only result in better educational performance but in greatly improved health and well-being for future Scottish citizens. They challenge the deeply-ingrained cultural acceptance, throughout Scotland and the rest of the UK, that formal instruction in the three Rs (reading, 'riting and 'rithmetic) should begin at the age of four or five – at least a year before other European countries.

Books can be ordered from www.postcardsfromscotland.co.uk or from www.amazon.co.uk Kindle editions are also available for some titles.